MANUFACTURING ENGINEERING DIPLOMA & ENGINEERING MCQ

MANOJ DOLE

Made with ♥ on the Notion Press Platform
www.notionpress.com

Contents

Foreword *v*

Preface *vii*

1. Manufacturing Engineering Hand Tools & Measuring Instruments Theory 1
2. Manufacturing Engineering Machines Theory 17
3. Manufacturing Engineering Cnc Machine Theory 30
4. Manufacturing Engineering Drawing Theory 34
5. Manufacturing Engineering Autocad Theory 41
6. Manufacturing Engineering Computer Skill Theory 48
7. Manufacturing Engineering Mcq 58

Foreword

Manufacturing Engineering Diploma & Engineering MCQ is a simple Book for Manufacturing Diploma & Engineering Course, It contains objective questions with underlined & bold correct answers MCQ covering all topics including all about the latest & Important about Engineering Science, Computer Studies, Engineering Drawing and CADD, Workshop Technology, Production Planning, Manufacturing Processes, Industrial Automation, C++ Programming, Theory of Machines, Kinematics & Dynamics, Mechanical and Structural Engineering, Thermodynamic, Fluid and Process Engineering, Engineering Materials, CNC and CAD/CAM Technology, Engineering Perspectives & Skills, Industrial Management Studies (Engineering) and lots more.

We add new question answers with each new version. Please email us in case of any errors/omissions. This is arguably the largest and best e-Book for All engineering multiple choice questions and answers.

As a student you can use it for your exam prep. This e-Book is also useful for professors to refresh material.

Preface

This book may be purchased for educational, business, or sales promotional use. Online edition is also available for this title. For more information, contact our corporate/institutional sales department: [+919921582799] or [manojdole1@gmail.com]

While every precaution has been taken in the preparation of this book, the publisher and authors assume no responsibility for errors or omissions, or for damages resulting from the use of the information contained herein.

About the Author

MANOJ DOLE is an Engineer from reputed University. He is currently working with Government Industrial Training- Institute as a lecturer from last 12 Years. His interest include- Engineering Training Material, Invention & Engineering Practical- Knowledge etc.

CHAPTER ONE

Manufacturing Engineering Hand Tools & Measuring Instruments Theory

Download App | Online Test Exam | ITI Books | AutoCAD CAM | JOB & Apprentice

Online Theory | Computer Course | Trading Course | CNC Course | MSCIT Course

Shopping Business | Internet Business | Web Designing | Online Services | Top Sportsmans

Indian Army | Freedom Fighters | Top Scientists | Social Reformers | Motivational Speaker

Top Richest People | Join WhatsApp Group | Join Facebook Group | Like Facebook Page | PAN / Adhar / Licence Passport

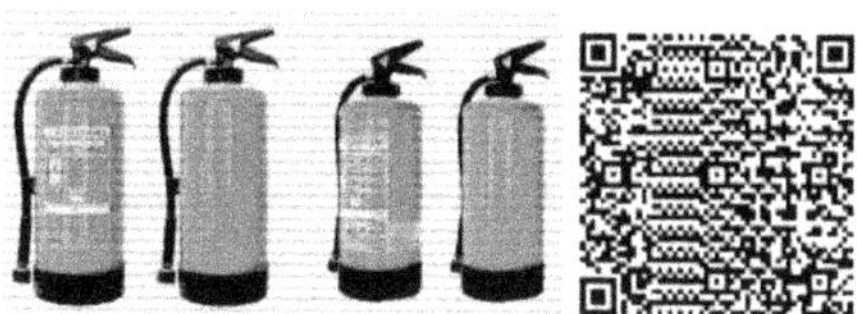

Fire extinguisher

Calliper

www.itibook.blogspot.com www.itiapp.blogspot.com www.ititests.blogspot.com

www.itibook.com

Hacksaw frame

Universal surface guage

Hammer

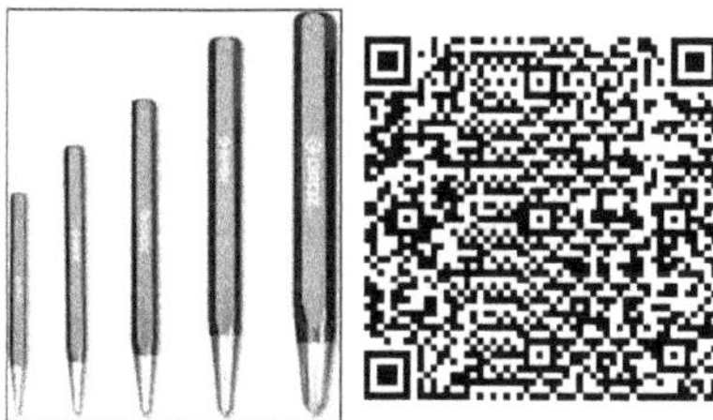

Centre punch

Bench vice

Files

Scraper

Surface Plate

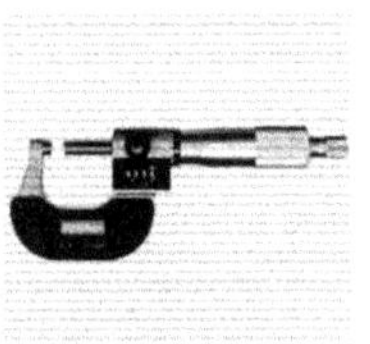

Outside Micrometer

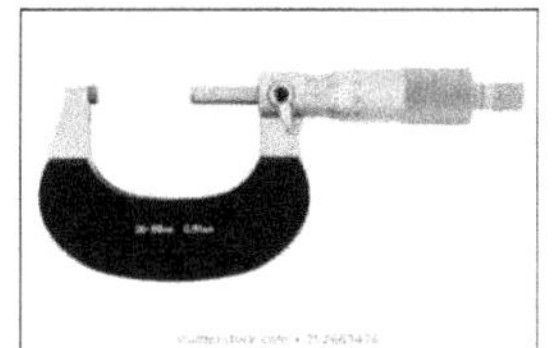

Micrometer

Depth micrometer

Vernier Calliper

Vernier bevel protractor

Drilling

Reamer

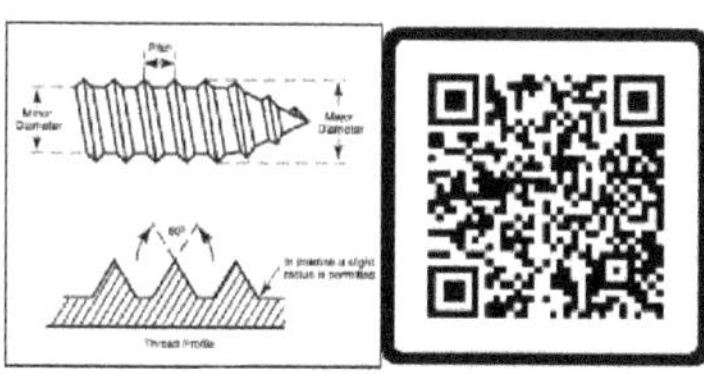

Thread

Tap Die

www.itibook.blogspot.com www.itiapp.blogspot.com www.ititests.blogspot.com

www.itibook.com

Grinding Wheel

Slip gauge

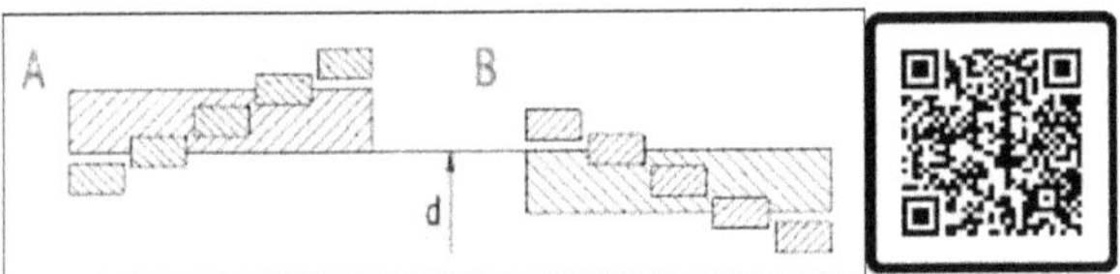

Limit fit tolerance

Lathe Machine

Lathe chuck

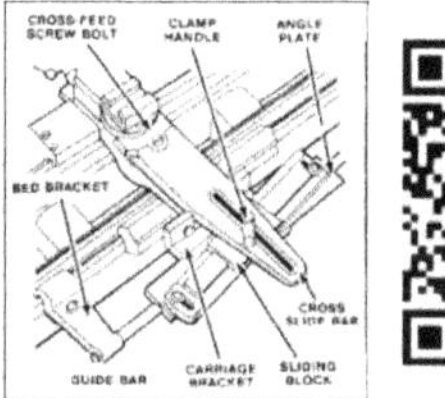

Taper turning attachment

taper ring gauge

screw pitch gauge

Gear

screw pitch gauge

Tap Die

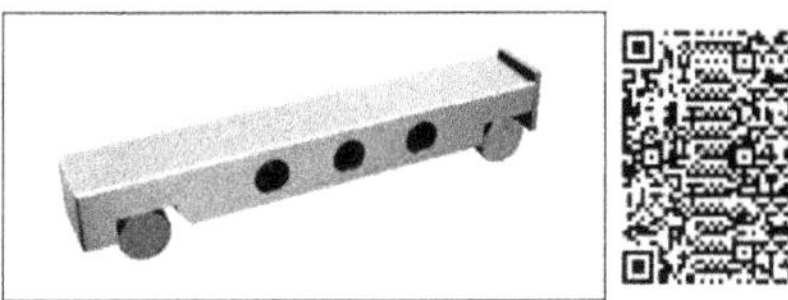

Sine bar

Slip gauge

Dial test indicator

Telescopic gauge

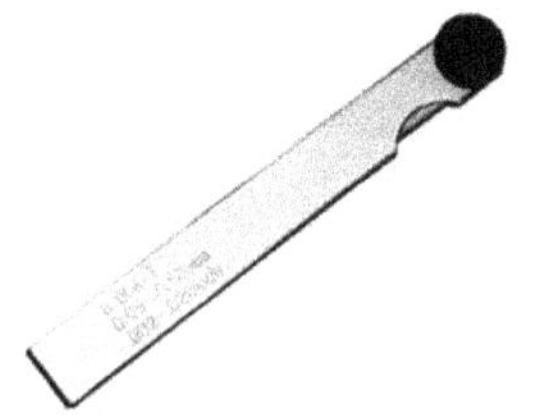

Feeler gauge

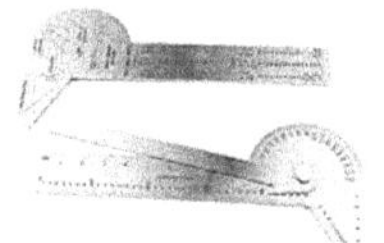

Centre gauge

Jig

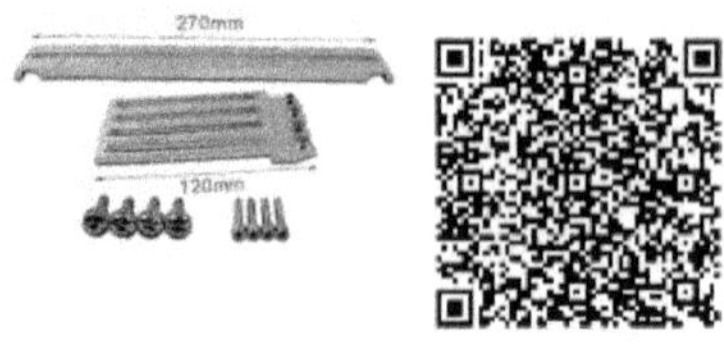

Fixture

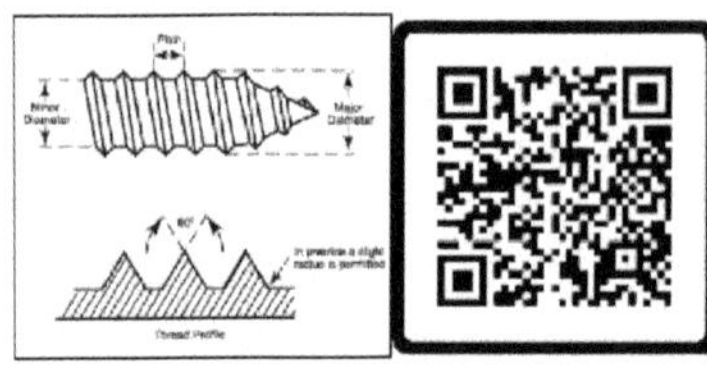

Thread

CHAPTER TWO

Manufacturing Engineering Machines Theory

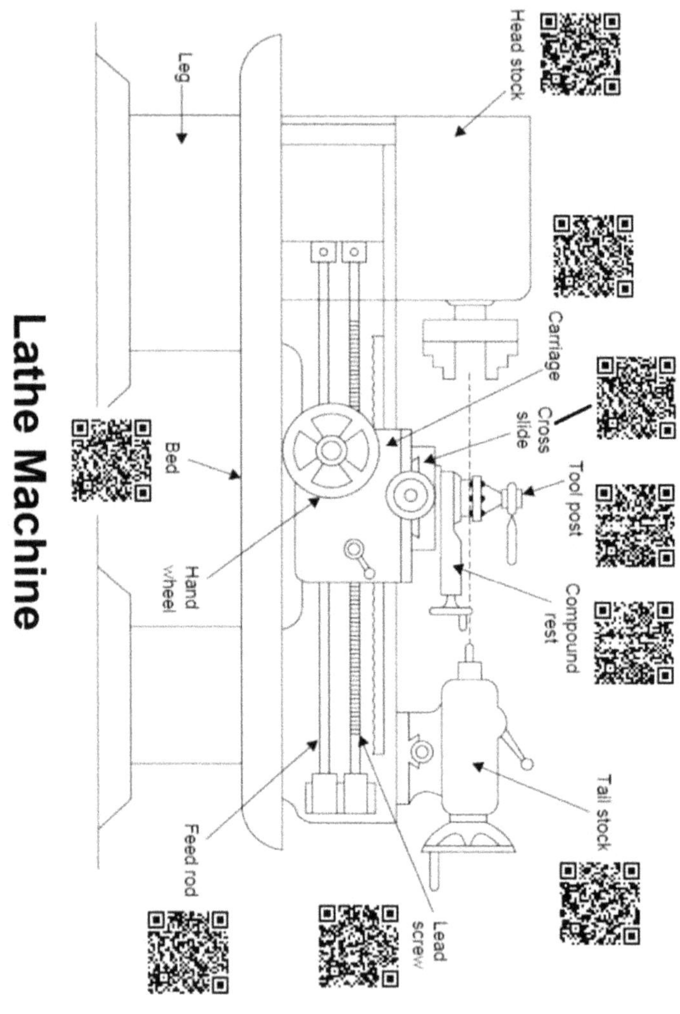
Lathe Machine
Head stock
Carriage
Cross slide
Tool post
Compound rest
Tail stock
Lead screw
Feed rod
Hand wheel
Bed
Leg

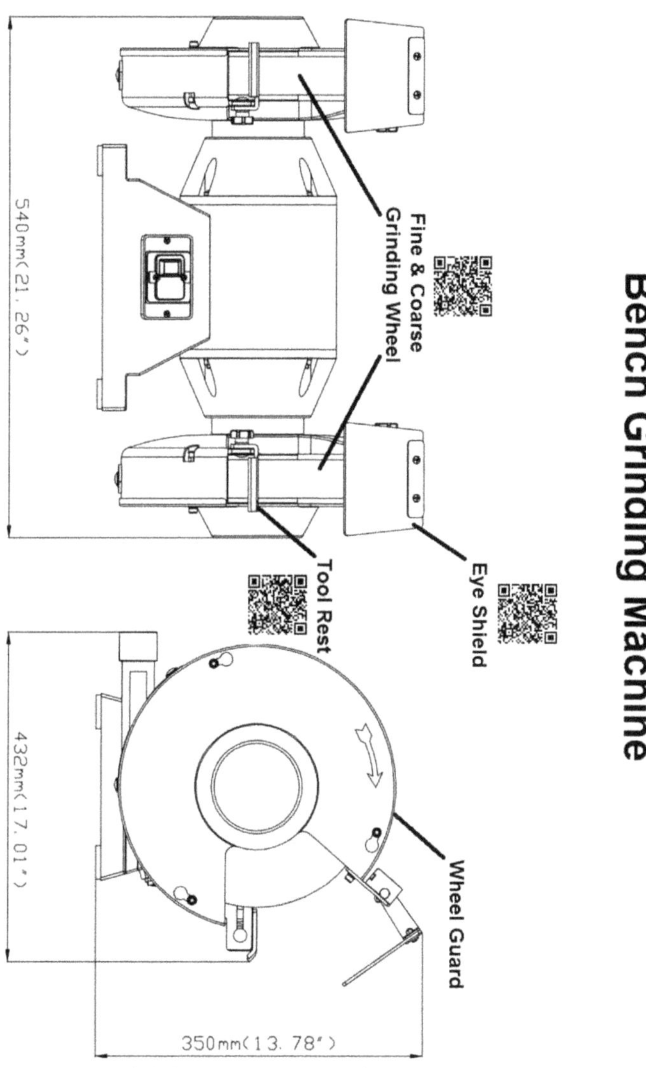
Bench Grinding Machine
Fine & Coarse Grinding Wheel
Eye Shield
Tool Rest
Wheel Guard
540mm(21.26")
432mm(17.01")
350mm(13.78")

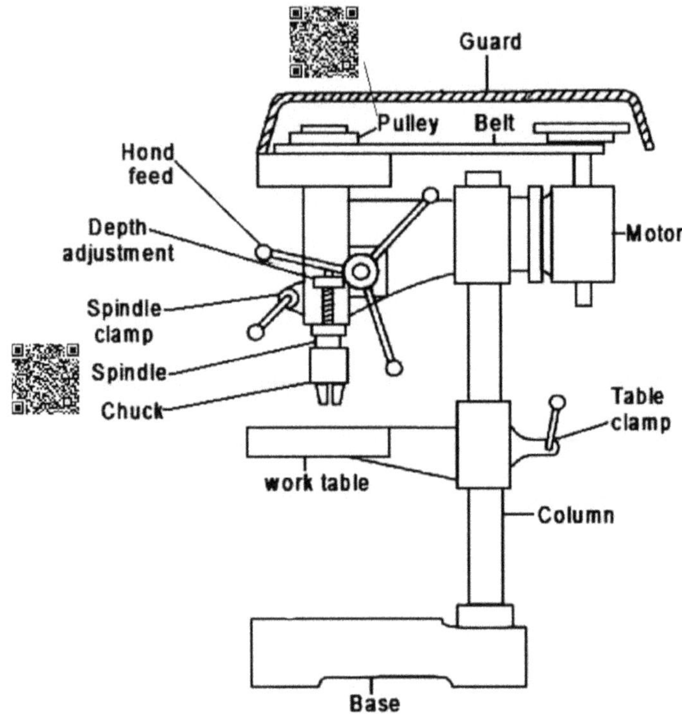

Piller Drilling Machine

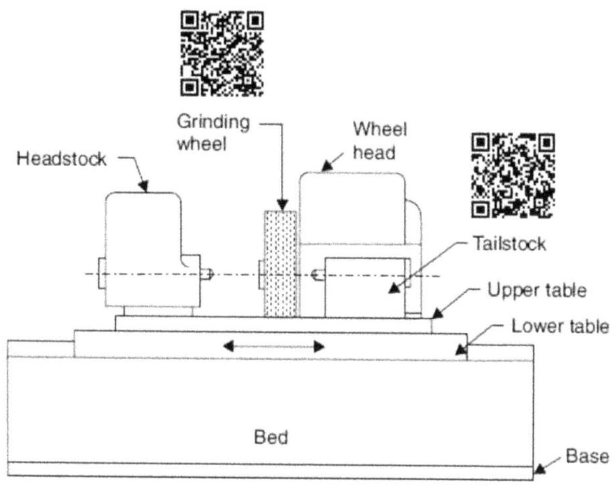

plain cylindrical grinder

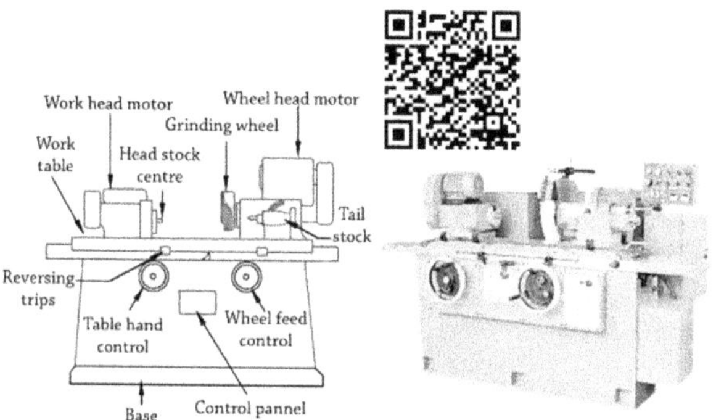

Cylindrical grinding machine

To study Different operations and parts of Surface Grinding Machine

SURFACE GRINDER

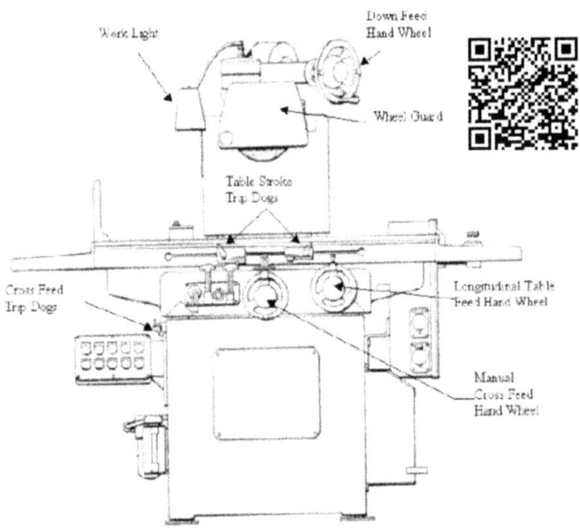

Surface grinding is used to produce a smooth finish on flat surfaces. It is a widely used abrasive machining process in which a spinning wheel covered in rough particles (grinding wheel) cuts

PLAIN OR HORIZONTAL MILLING MACHINE

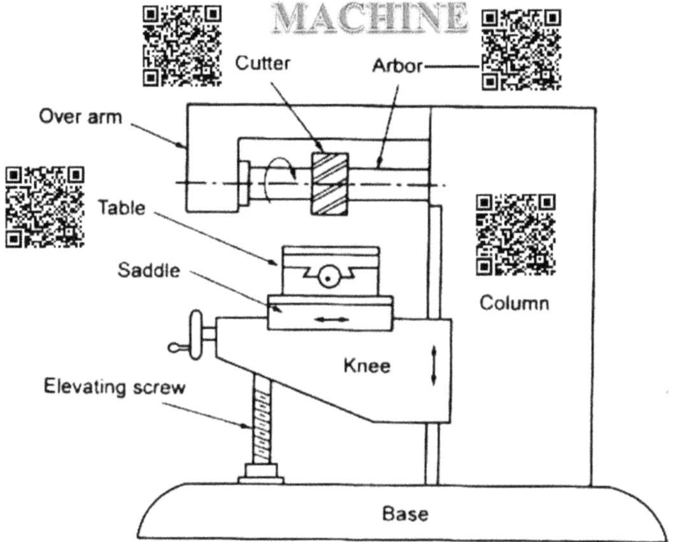

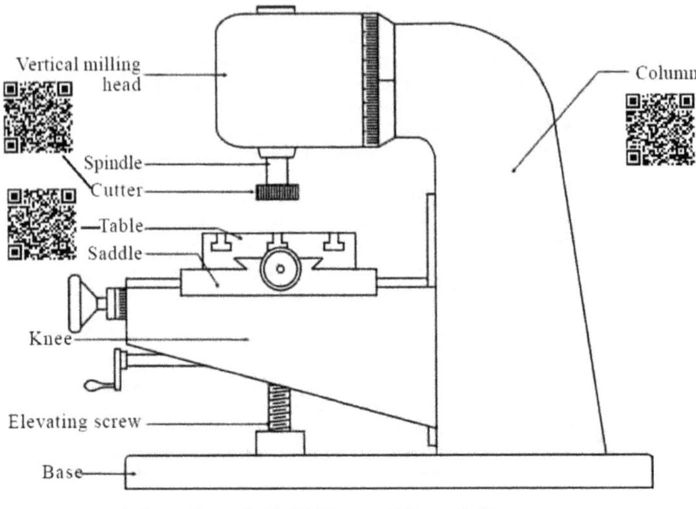

Vertical Milling Machine

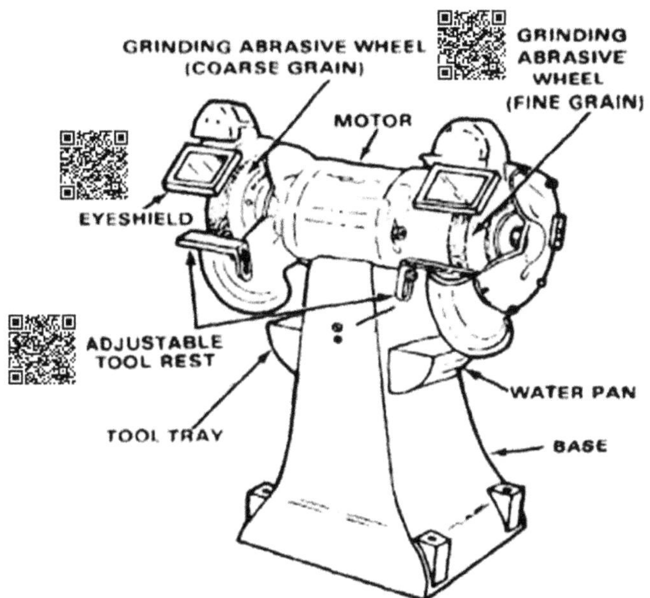

Pedastal Grinding Machine

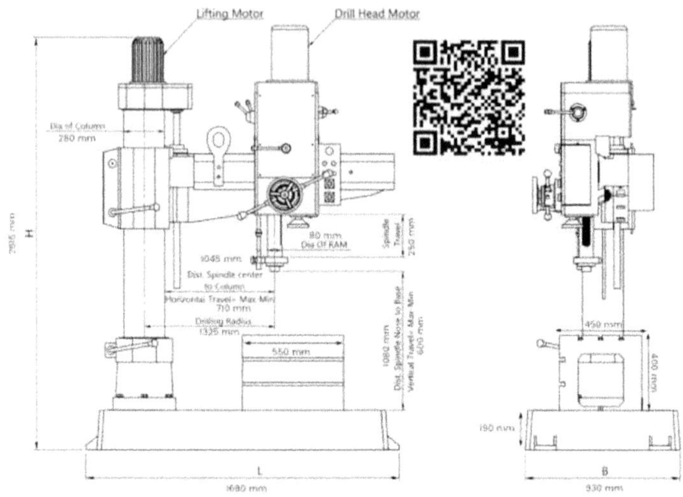

Radial Drilling Machine

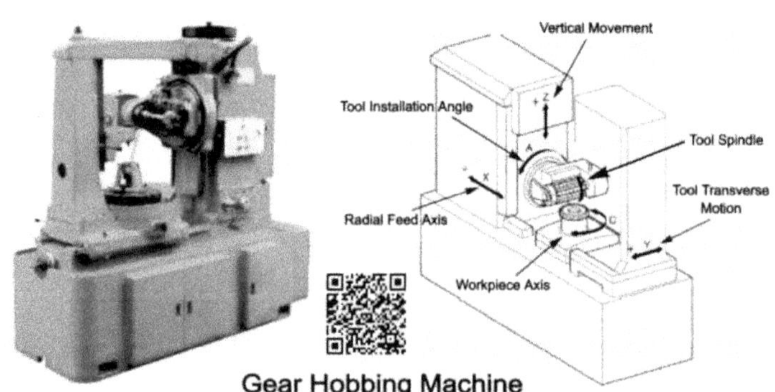

Gear Hobbing Machine

DOUBLE HOUSING PLANER

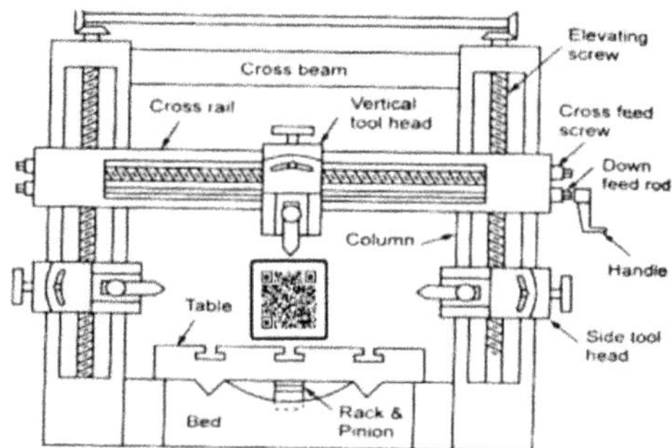

PIT PLANER

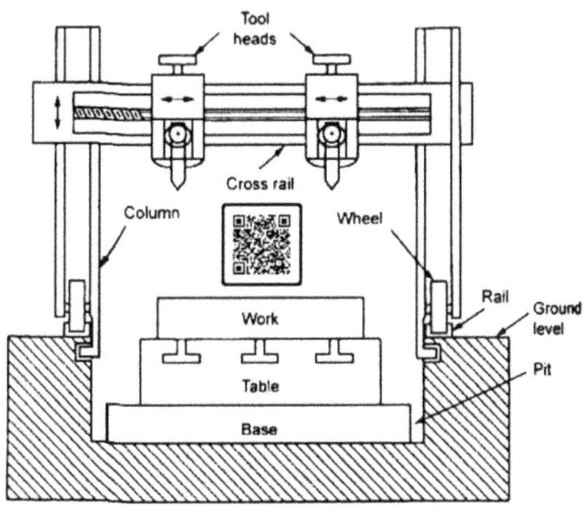

OPEN SIDE PLANER

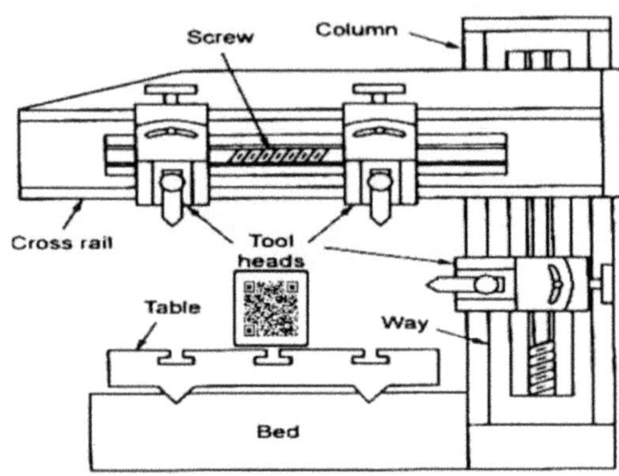

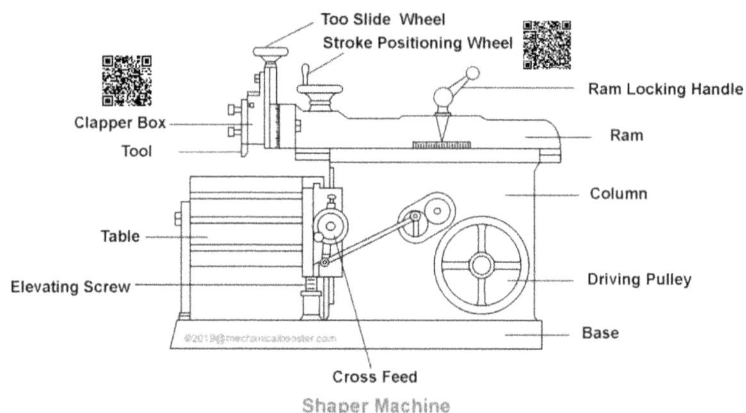

Shaper Machine

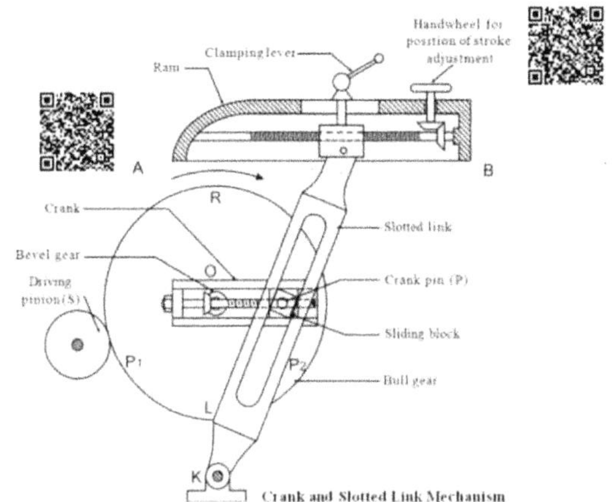

Crank and Slotted Link Mechanism

Quick Return Mechanism of Shaper Machine

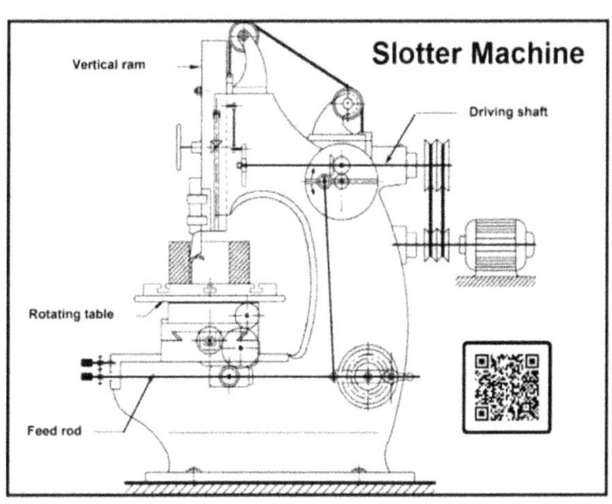

CHAPTER THREE

Manufacturing Engineering CNC Machine Theory

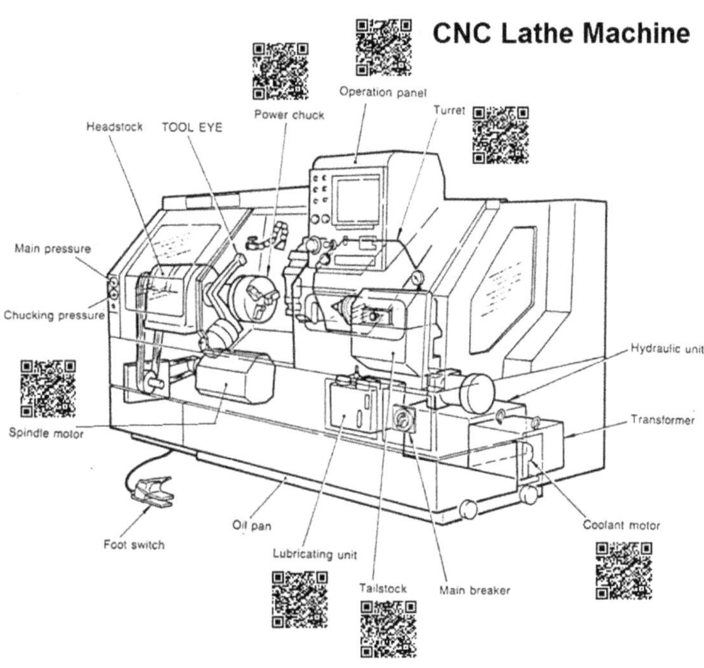
CNC Lathe Machine
Operation panel
Power chuck
Turret
Headstock
TOOL EYE
Main pressure
Chucking pressure
Hydraulic unit
Transformer
Spindle motor
Coolant motor
Oil pan
Foot switch
Lubricating unit
Tailstock
Main breaker

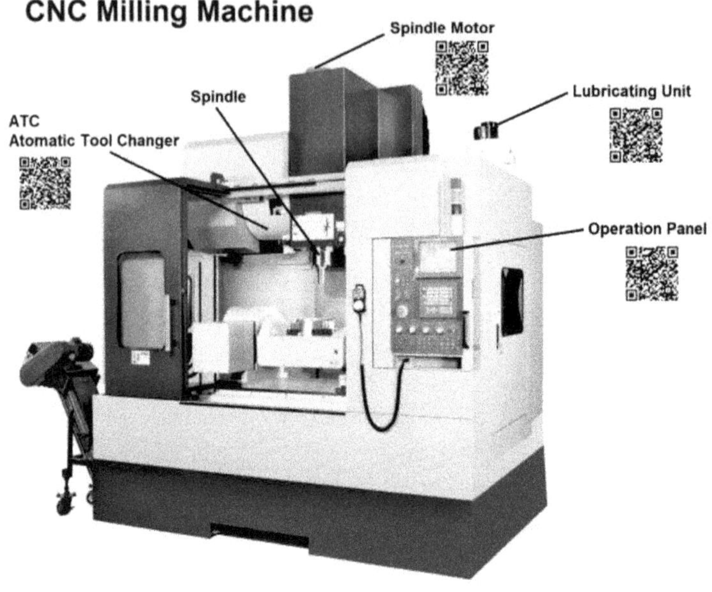

CNC Machine Lubrication

ATC Automatic Tool Changer

Animation & Video

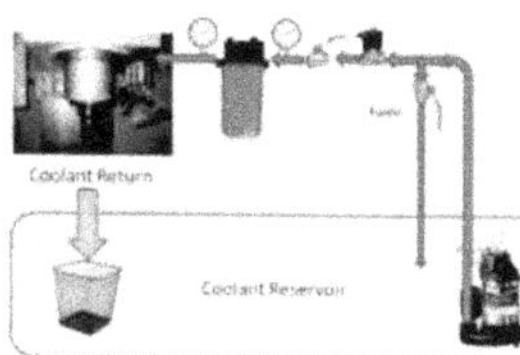

CNC Coolant Pump

Animation & Video

CHAPTER FOUR

Manufacturing Engineering Drawing Theory

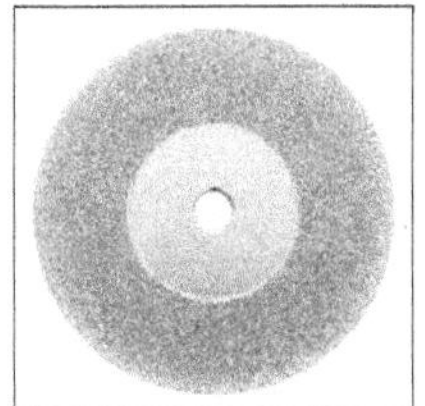

Grinding

Fire extinguisher

French curve in drawing

Set square in drawing

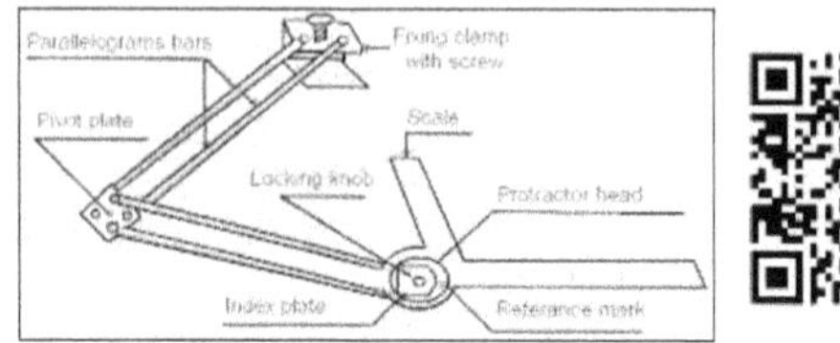

Mini drafter in drawing

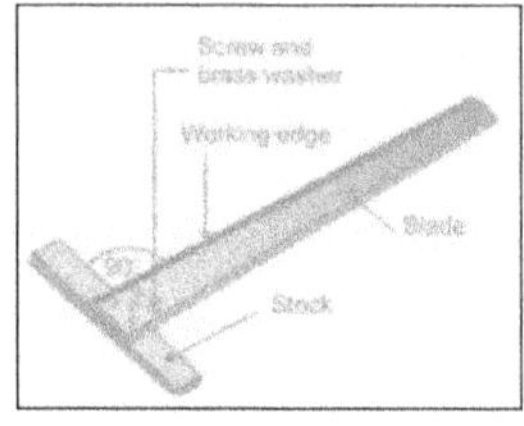

T - square in drawing

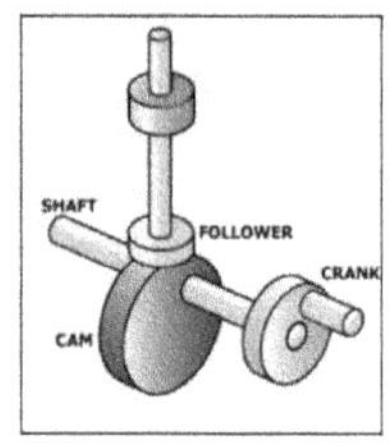

Cams in engine

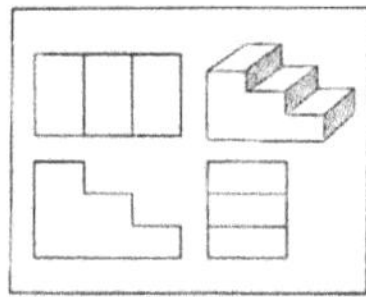

Orthographic projection in drawing

Third angle projection drawing

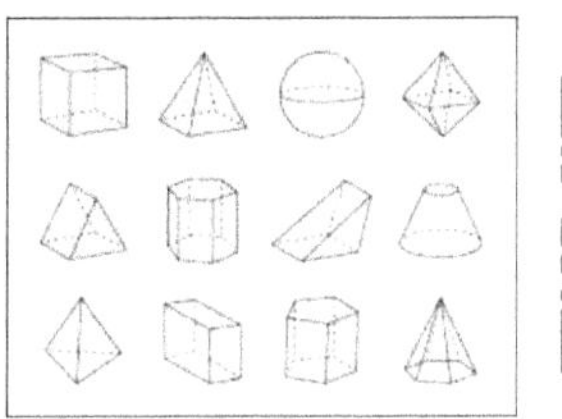

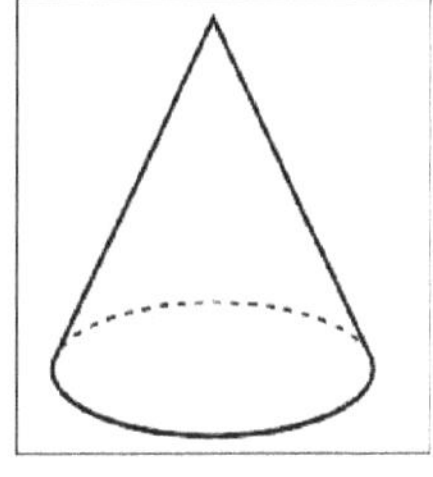

Cone in engineering drawing

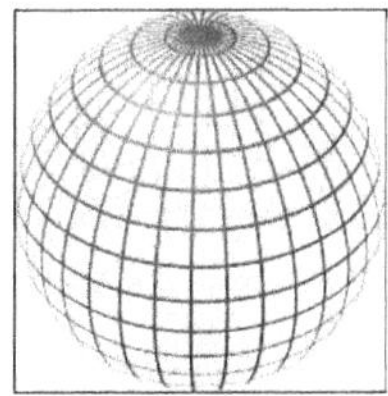

Sphere in drawing

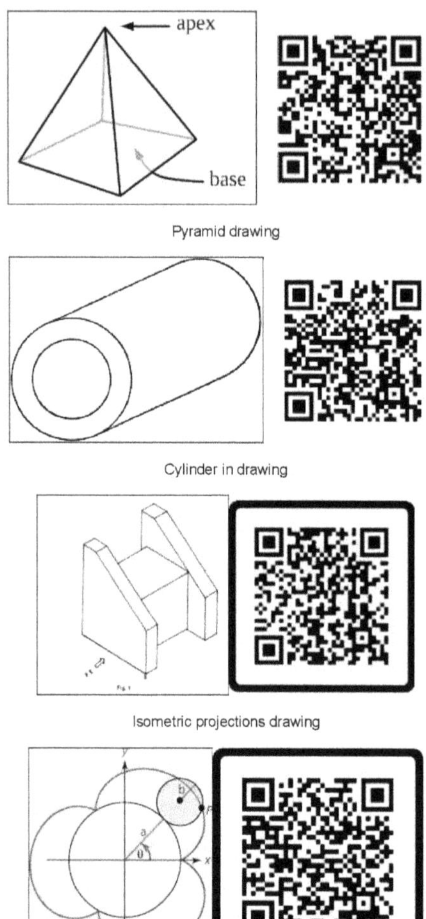

Pyramid drawing

Cylinder in drawing

Isometric projections drawing

Curves engineering drawing

Sectional views in drawing

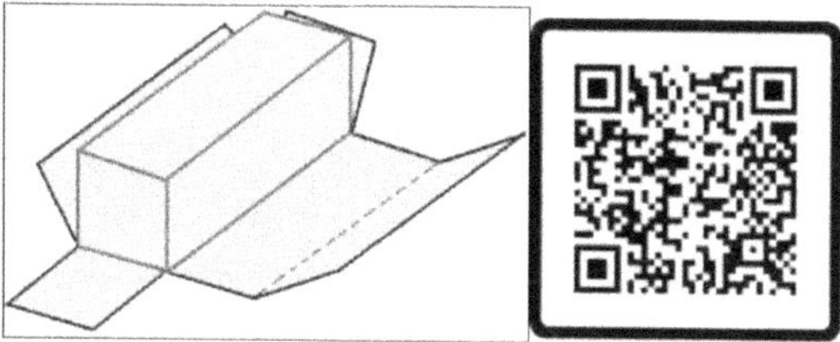

Development of surfaces in drawing

Hexagonal plane in drawing

Polyhedron in drawing

First Angle projection method in drawing

Springs in drawing

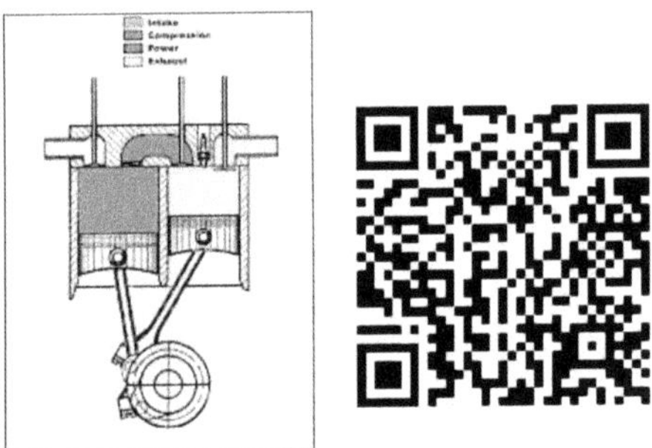

Engine in vehicle

CHAPTER FIVE

Manufacturing Engineering AutoCAD Theory

AutoCAD Command Shortcut Keys

CTRL+Q	Exit public consciousness
CTRL+R	Remove ornamentation
CTRL+S	Save as Stainless Steel
CTRL+SHFT+S	Save as a better design (ie. Titanium)
CTRL+T	Toggles Talent (requires administrative access)
CTRL+V	Value Engineer (reduces scale by 78%)
CTRL+SHFT+V	Pastes data from ArchRecord as Block
CTRL+X	Begin unpaid Furlough
CTRL+Y	Repeats last award winning design
CTRL+Z	Speed dial Zaha Hadid
CTRL+ZZZ	Sleep (not applicable)
CTRL+[	Cancels current schedule
CTRL+\	Cancels current budget
CTRL+ANGST+DEL	(no action)

F1	Displays Help wanted sign in café window
F2	Toggles all text to Helvetica
F3	Toggles Oh-SNAP
F4	Toggles MODERNISM
F5	Toggles ISOLATION
F6	Toggles CORBUSIER
F7	Toggles IRRELEVANT GRID
F8	Toggles ORTHO MODE (should always be on)
F9	Toggles POSTMODERNISM (should always be off)
F10	Toggles NORWAY
F11	Toggles ARROGANCE

AutoCAD Command Shortcut Keys

ALT+F8	Delete detail
ALT+F11	Add white
CTRL+1	Simplify Palette
CTRL+2	Remove Interior Design Palette
CTRL+3	Complicate Construction Process
CTRL+4	Add 4 extraneous sheets
CTRL+5	Remove Client's color Palette
CTRL+6	Remove Client's wife's color Palette (must press hard)
CTRL+7	Markup Set for interns (with only circles and question marks)
CTRL+A	Selects objects in drawing that aren't really needed
CTRL+B	Sends resume to B.I.G.
CTRL+SHIFT+B	Shifts blame to Consultants
CTRL+C	Copies angst to Clipboard
CTRL+SHFT+C	Copies angst to Clipboard with Base Point (ie. Finland)
CTRL+D	Delete relevance
CTRL+E	Cycles through design ideologies
CTRL+F	Flatten all roofs
CTRL+G	Insert 9-square Grid
CTRL+H	Insert Awesomeness
CTRL+L	Adds "Le" in front of all nouns
CTRL+K	Justify design concept
CTRL+L	Left justify design concept
CTRL+M	Less and/or more
CTRL+N	Insert new idea (bills client for additional time required)
CTRL+O	Opens ArchDaily.com
CTRL+P	Prints unemployment check

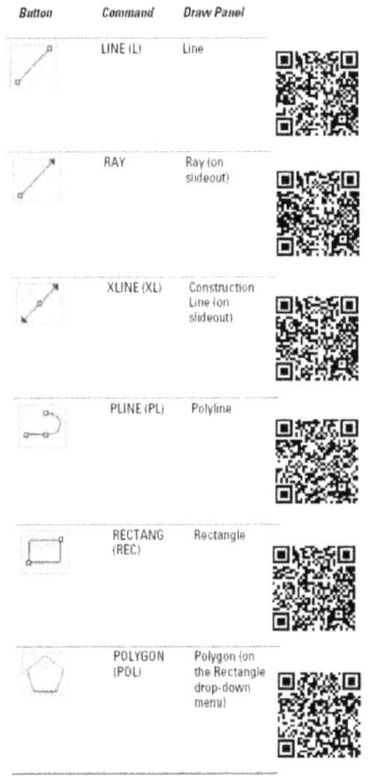

Button	Command	Draw Panel
	LINE (L)	Line
	RAY	Ray (on slideout)
	XLINE (XL)	Construction Line (on slideout)
	PLINE (PL)	Polyline
	RECTANG (REC)	Rectangle
	POLYGON (POL)	Polygon (on the Rectangle drop-down menu)

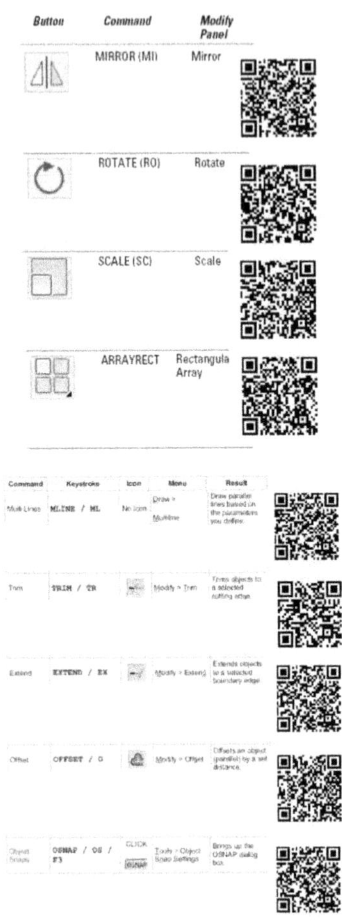

Button	Command	Modify Panel
	MIRROR (MI)	Mirror
	ROTATE (RO)	Rotate
	SCALE (SC)	Scale
	ARRAYRECT	Rectangula Array

Command	Keystroke	Icon	Menu	Result
Multi Lines	MLINE / ML	No Icon	Draw > Multiline	Draw parallel lines based on the parameters you define.
Trim	TRIM / TR		Modify > Trim	Trims objects to a selected cutting edge.
Extend	EXTEND / EX		Modify > Extend	Extends objects to a selected boundary edge.
Offset	OFFSET / O		Modify > Offset	Offsets an object (parallel) by a set distance.
Object Snaps	OSNAP / OS / F3	CLICK OSNAP	Tools > Object Snap Settings	Brings up the OSNAP dialog box.

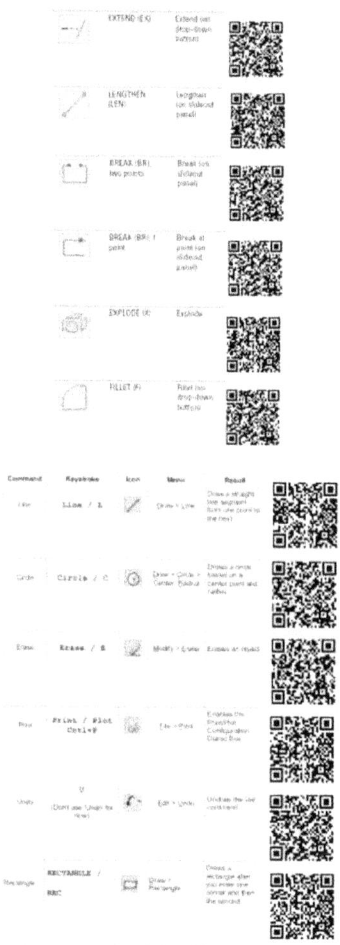

Icon	Command	Description	QR
	EXTEND (EX)	Extend (on drop-down button)	
	LENGTHEN (LEN)	Lengthen (on slideout panel)	
	BREAK (BR) two points	Break (on slideout panel)	
	BREAK (BR) 1 point	Break at point (on slideout panel)	
	EXPLODE (X)	Explode	
	FILLET (F)	Fillet (on drop-down button)	

Command	Keystroke	Icon	Menu	Result	
Line	Line / L		Draw > Line	Draws a straight line segment from one point to the next	
Circle	Circle / C		Draw > Circle > Center, Radius	Draws a circle based on a center point and radius	
Erase	Erase / E		Modify > Erase	Erases an object	
Plot	Print / Plot Ctrl+P		File > Print	Enables the Plot/Print Configuration Dialog Box	
Undo	U (Don't use 'Undo' for now)		Edit > Undo	Undoes the last command	
Rectangle	RECTANGLE / REC		Draw > Rectangle	Draws a rectangle after you enter one corner and then the second	

Button	Command	Modify Panel
	ERASE (E)	Erase
	MOVE (M)	Move
	COPY (CO or CP)	Copy
	STRETCH (S)	Stretch
	ARRAYPOLAR	Polar Array
	ARRAYPATH	Path Array
	ARRAYEDIT	Edit Array (on slideout panel)
	OFFSET (O)	Offset
	TRIM (TR)	Trim (on drop-down button)

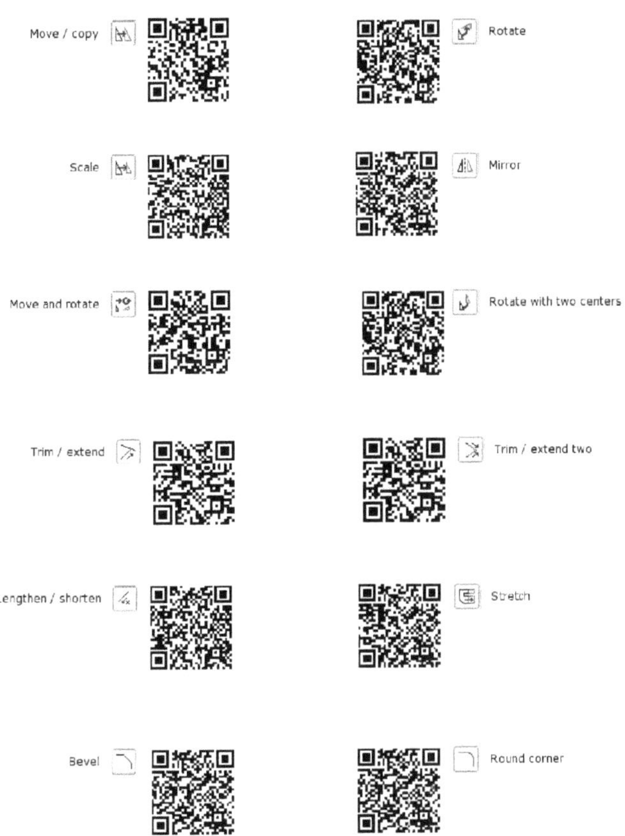
Move / copy
Rotate
Scale
Mirror
Move and rotate
Rotate with two centers
Trim / extend
Trim / extend two
Lengthen / shorten
Stretch
Bevel
Round corner

CHAPTER SIX

Manufacturing Engineering Computer Skill Theory

COMPUTER PARTS
COMPUTER
MOUSE
KEY BOARD
SCREEN / MONITOR
FLASH DRIVE
TOWER
COMPACT DISC
LAPTOP
PRINTER
SCANNER
CARTRIDGES
WEB CAM

COMPUTER PARTS
SPEAKER
HEADPHONES
SMARTPHONE
TABLET / I-PAD
MICROPHONE
WIRELESS ROUTER
MP3 PLAYER
JOYSTICK / GAME

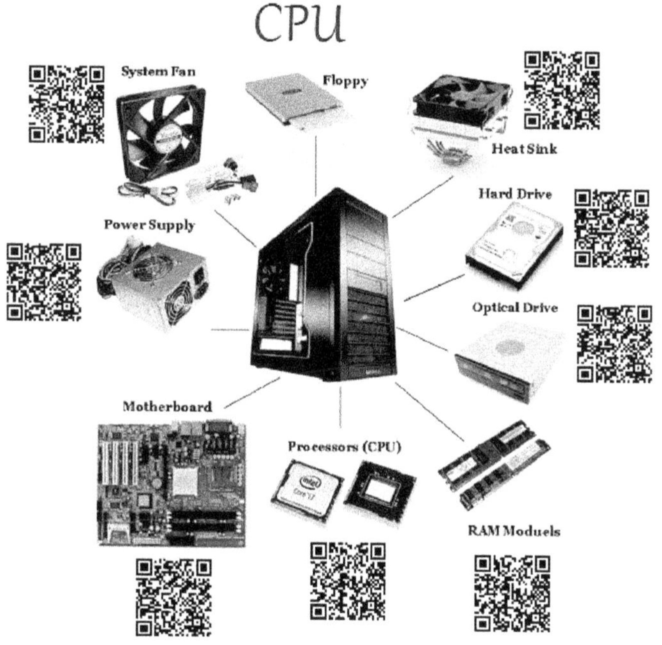

Computer CPU Hardware Components

Motherboard Hardware Components

Excel Basic Functions

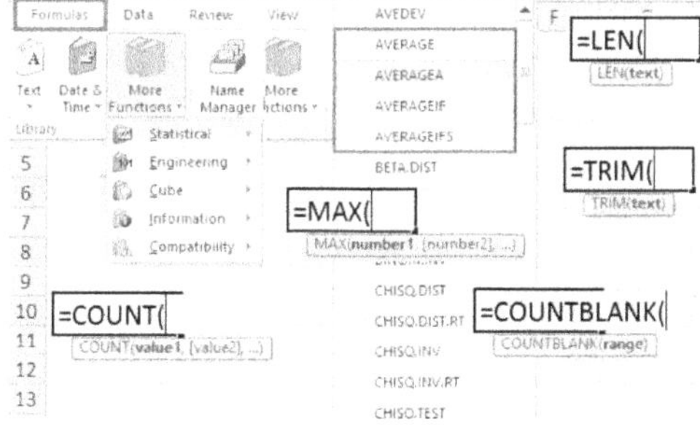

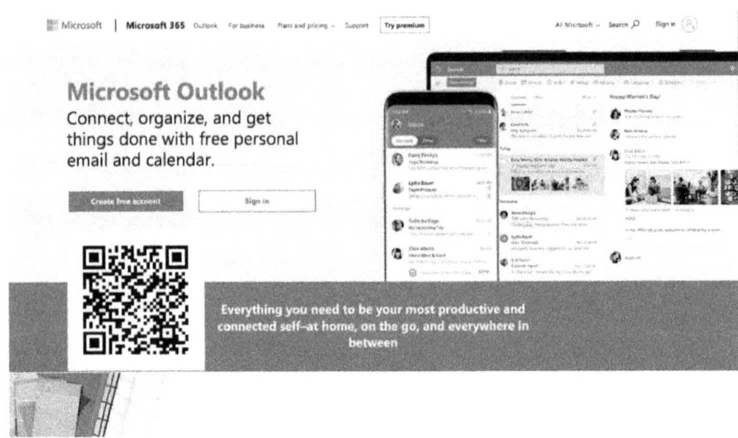
Microsoft | Microsoft 365
Try premium
Microsoft Outlook
Connect, organize, and get things done with free personal email and calendar.
Sign in
Everything you need to be your most productive and connected self–at home, on the go, and everywhere in between

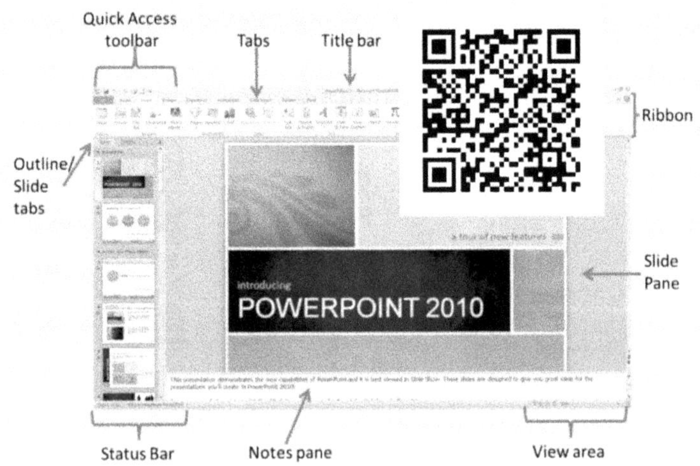
Quick Access toolbar
Tabs
Title bar
Ribbon
Outline/ Slide tabs
Slide Pane
introducing
POWERPOINT 2010
Status Bar
Notes pane
View area

MS Paint

Microsoft
FEATURES OF
MS WORD
IN HINDI
W
• WHAT IS MS WORD
• HISTORY OF MS WORD
• FEATURES OF MS WORD

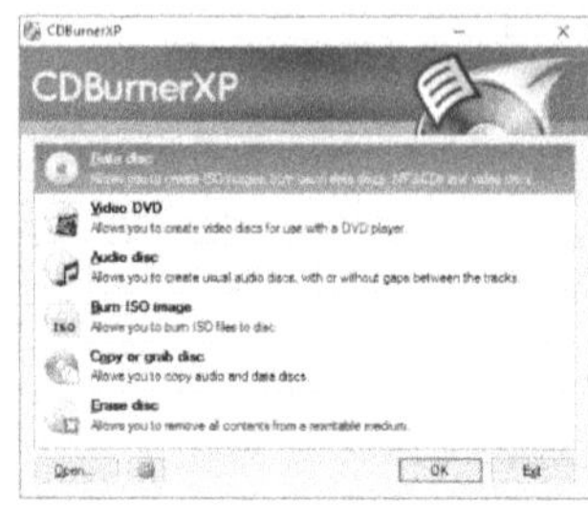
CDBurnerXP
Video DVD
Allows you to create video discs for use with a DVD player
Audio disc
Burn ISO image
Allows you to burn ISO files to disc
Copy or grab disc
Allows you to copy audio and data discs
Erase disc
OK
Exit

DRIVER
Scan
ALLXPSOFT.COM

Top Linux OS
debian
ZORIN OS
KALI

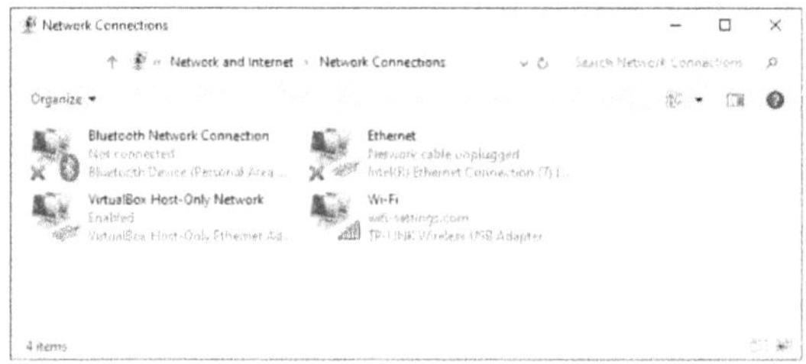
Network Connections
Network and Internet
Network Connections
Organize
Bluetooth Network Connection
Ethernet
VirtualBox Host-Only Network
Wi-Fi
4 items

Software Installation

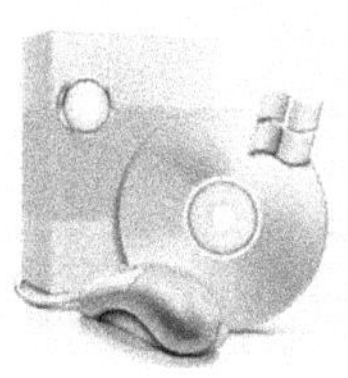

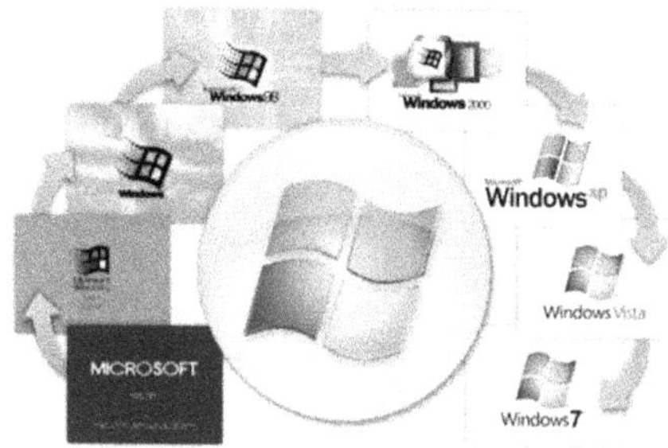

CHAPTER SEVEN

Manufacturing Engineering MCQ

Safety Precaution in Manufacturing Engineering

01] In case of bleeding, take treatment Of

A] spray cold water

B] Bandage immediately -----]

C] Enquire about the accident thought treatment

D] cold 3" and rest

02] in case of an accident, the victim should im

A] Asked to take rest

C] Attended immediately

D] leave him

03] First aid is given to an injured or ill person primarily....

A] Save life

B] Prevent further deterioration of the muff's

C] Give best possible comfort

D] All of these

04] Colour code for Bins for waste paper segregation is -----

A] blue Colour

B] Yellow Colour

C] Red Colour

D] Green Colour

05] In Japanese Seiko stands for -------------

A] Shine

B] Sort

C] Standardize

D] Sustain

06] Benefit of SS system is ------

A] Increase in productivity

B] Increase in quality

C] Reduction in wastage of time

<u>D] All of these</u>

07] Safety is -----------

A] nobody's business

<u>B] every bodise business</u>

C] Some bodies business

D] The organization business

08] For basic categories of safety signs are available The meaning of"prohibition" sign ----

<u>A] shows it must not be done</u>

B] Shows what must be done

C] Warns the hazard or danger

D] Gives information of safety provision

09] Which one is a workshop safety?

<u>A] Keep shop floor clean and free from grease, oil or other slippery materials</u>

B] Stop the machine before changing the speed

C] Don't use cracked or chipped tools

D] Don't try to stop a running machine with hand

10] In Personal Protect Equipment (PPE] HELMET is used to

<u>A] protect head</u>

B] Protect eyes

C] Protect hands

D] Protect ears

11] Which of the following belongs to general safety?

A Have a worker in good attitude

B] The work clean and clear

C] Concentrate on your work

<u>D] Keep the floor and gangways clean and clear</u>

12] While grinding, which is used to protect the eyes?

A] Dark green glass

B] Mask

C] Sun glasses

<u>D] Safety goggles</u>

13] Which of the following is done for machine safety?

<u>A] Check the oil level before starting the machine</u>

B] Do things in a methodical way

C] Keep the floor and gangways clean and clear

D] Don't use dies and scarves

14] ln Personal Protect Equipment (PPE], 'sleeves' is used to protect ----------

A] Face

B] Eyes

C] Ears

D] Hands

15] ABC stands for --------------

A] Automatic Breathing Control

B] Automatic Blood Control

C] Airway Breathing Circulation

D] Automatic Blood Circulation

16] To put off"Class B" fire, the types of fire extinguisher used is ....]

A] dry power

B] Carbon dioxide

C] Jet of water

D] Foam type

17] Which type of fire extinguisher is used to put off general fire?

A] Water type Extinguisher

B] Foam type Extinguisher

C] Dry chemical powder Extinguisher

D] Carbon dioxide (C02] Extinguisher

Hand Tools in Manufacturing Engineering

18] One micrometer (U] is equal to...

A] 0.1mm

B] 0.01mm

C] 0.001mm

D] 0.0001mm

19] Name the tool used to make and finish the leak proof joints of a pipe T joint

A] groover

B] setting hammer

C] creasing hammer

D] round bottom stake

20] Portion of the hammer used for fixing the handle is...

A] Face

B] Peen

C] Cheek

D] Eye hole

21] Weight of the hammer for the marking purpose is...

A] 250g

B] 500g

C] 1 kg

D] 2 kgs

22] To cut out small apertures which punch and die type of machine is used?

A] shear type nibbler

B] punch type nibbler

C] circular cutting machine

D] guillotine shearing machine

23] Scribers are made of...

A] Mild steel

B] High carbon steel

C] Brass

D] Cast iron

24] The size of an engineer's vice is specified by the...

A] Length of the movable jaw

B] Width of the jaws

C] Height of the vice

D] Maximum opening of the jaws

vice Bench vice

Bench Vice

25] The form of thread used in carpenters vice is...

A] Square

B] Acme thread

C] Sawtooth Thread

D] Knuckle thread

26] The convexity of files helps...

A] To file concave surfaces

B] To file convex surfaces

C] To prevent rounding of edges of work

D] The file to become straight when pressure is applied

27]] Name the instrument used to check the perpendicularity of the branch pipe with the main pipe of a pipe T joint

A] protractor

B] try square

C] spirit level

D] straight edge

28] The caliper meant for measuring the width of a slot is...

A] Odd leg caliper

B] Outside caliper

C] Jenny caliper

D] Inside calliper

29] The included angle of the groove of 'V' block is always....

A] 45◦

B] 60◦

C] 90◦

D] 120◦

v blocks

v block

'V' blocks

30] 'V' blocks are available in grades of...

A] A & B

B] A,B & C

C] 1,2 & 3

D] 1 & 2

31] 'V' blocks of grade 'B' are made of

A] Cast iron

B] Mild steel

C] Steel

D] Cast steel

32] 'V' block 50/5-40 A is used for holding jobs of diameter

A] Ø 50 mm

B] Ø 5 to Ø 50 mm

C] Ø 5 to Ø 40 mm

D] Ø 40 mm

33] The reason for using cast iron in making 'V' blocks

A] to increase the weight of the block

B] to reduce the cost

C] to reduce the friction

D] to get a good appearance

34] For cutting thin tubing, the most suitable pitch of the hacksaw blade is...

A] 1.8mm

B] 1.4mm

C] 1mm

D] 0.8mm

35] For cutting solid brass, the most suitable pitch of the hacksaw blade is...

A] 1.8mm

B] 1.4mm

C] 1mm

D] 0.8mm

36] A new hacksaw blade after a few strokes becomes loose because of the...

A] Stretching of the blade

B] Wing-nut threads being worn out

C] Wrong pitch of the blade

D] Improper selection of the set of saws.

37] While cutting small diameter pipes, it is advisable to watch regularly and ensure that...

A] The cut is along the curved line

B] More saw teeth are in contract

C] The work is not overheated

D] Proper balancing of hacksaw is maintained

Drilling in Manufacturing Engineering

38] If the drill runs untrue, it will

A] get too hot

B] cut undersize

C] distort the spindle

D] cut an oversized hole

39] Running the drill too fast many result in

A] spoiling the cutting edge

B] poor surface finish

C] twisting the tang

D] drilling an oval hole

40] A drill with worn land will
A] drill hole oversize
B] drill hole undersize
C] run out of centre
D] drill an accurate hole
41] The morse taper provided on drills used on lathe ranges between
A] MT1 to MT5
B] MT1 to MT4
C] MT0 to MT5
D] MT0 to MT4
42] Feeding the small drill too fast into the work may result in
A] breaking the drill
B] bending the drill
C] cutting an oval shape hole
D] increased production
43] The drill size for a M 20 tap is
A] 17.5 mm
B] 18 mm
C] 18.5 mm
D] 19 mm
44] The taper shank drills are held on the machine by means of...
A] Chucks
B] Sleeves
C] Drift
D] Vice
45] Drill chucks are fitted on the drilling machine spindle by means of a...
A] Knurled ring
B] Arbor
C] Drift
D] Pinion and key

drill chuck

drilling

Drill Chuck

46] The Morse taper provided on drills ranges between...

A] MT 1 to MT 5

B] MT 1 to MT 4

C] MT 0 to MT 5

D] MT 0 to MT 4

47] A drift is used for...

A] Drawing a drill location

B] Fixing chuck on the machine spindle

C] Removing a broken drill from the work

D] Removing the drill from the machine spindle

48] When the taper shank of the drill is larger than the machine spindle, the device to hold the drill is a...

A] Drill sleeve

B] Taper socket

C] Drill drift

D] Chuck and key

49] A special feature of the radial drilling machine is...

A] It can be used for drilling with a H.S.S] drill

B] Table can be moved and set at any position

C] A variety of speeds is available

D] **The spindle can be brought to any position**

50] The point angle of drills depends on...

A] The size of the drill

B] The type of machine

C] **The material of the work**

D] The RPM of the drill

51] The point angle for a standard drill is...

A] 60°

B] 108°

C] **118°**

D] 135°

52] The helical angle determines the...

A] Cutting angle

B] Chew angle

C] **Rake angle**

D] Lip angle

53] The clearance angle of the drill is between...

A] 3° to 5°

B] **8° to 12°**

C] 12° to 20°

D] 15° to 20°

54] The relief angle provided behind the cutting edge is called the..

A] Point angle

B] Chisel edge angle

C] Helix angle

D] **Clearance angle**

55] A set of number drill series consists of drills in the following ranges] Indicate the correct range

A] 1 to 40

B] 1 to 50

C] **1 to 80**

D] 1 to 100

56] In the number drill series, the smallest drill size is...

A] 0.1 mm

B] 0.35 mm
C] 0.5 mm
D] 0.52 mm
57] In the number drill series, the largest drill size is...
A] 102 mm
B] 5.791 mm
C] 5.613 mm
D] 5.410 mm
58] In the letter drill series, the size of the drill 'A' is equal to ...
A] 13 mm
B] 6.08 mm
C] 6.045 mm
D] 5.944 mm
59] In the letter drill series, the largest drill size is equal to...
A] 10.33 mm
B] 10.490 mm
C] 12.01 mm
D] 15.00 mm
60] In a remote place (no electricity available] a rail track is to be drilled] Choose the right drilling machine
A] Radial drilling machine
B] Pillar drilling machine
C] Ratchet drilling machine
D] Sensitive drilling Machine
61] A drilling machine used by a carpenter for cabinet making is a...
A] Ratchet drilling machine
B] Radial drilling machine
C] Breast drilling machine
D] Sensitive drilling machine
62] Surface plates are made of...
A] High grade cast steel
B] Fine-grained cast iron
C] Alloy steels
D] Wrought iron
63] The drill size for a M 20 tap is
A] 17.5 mm
B] 18 mm
C] 18.5 mm

D] 19 mm

64] Tapping is mostly done to produce

A] external 'V' thread

B] internal 'V' thread

C] external square thread

D] internal square thread

65] The drill size for tapping is

A] more than the tap size

B] less than the tap size

C] equal to the tap size

D] either more or less than the tap size

66] which one of the following is the most suitable tap for lathe work?

A] spiral tap

B] machine tap

C] hand tap

D] left hand tap

67] A die is turned with a

A] die wrench

B] diestock

C] die plate

D] die handle

68] A tumbler gear unit has

A] a single gear

B] two gears

C] three gears

D] four gears

69] The cutting edge of a solid tool is made of

A] carbon steel

B] mild steel

C] super high speed steel

D] stelite

70] The tip of a cemented carbide threading tool is

A] brazed

B] welded

C] soldered

D] clamped to the shank

71] Tool will rub against the work surfaces and the cutting force increases when..

A] The clearance angle is more
B] The clearance angel is less
C] The rake angle is more
D] The rake angle is less
72] Formation of a chip while cutting is based on the...
A] Rake angle of the tool
B] Clearance angle of the tool
C] Wedge angle of the tool
D] Clearance and wedge angle of the tool
73] The suitable cutting fluid for drilling mild steel in a drilling machine is...
A] Synthetic soluble oil
B] Neat oil
C] Distilled water
D] Soluble oil
74] Centre drilling is an operation of...
A] Drilling and countersinking
B] Drilling and counter boring
C] Marking the centre location before drilling
D] Enlarging the diameter of a hole
75] Shaft ends are centre drilled for...
A] Supporting jobs between centres
B] Lubricating the dead centre
C] Reducing the weight
D] Assisting counter boring
76] The Centre drill size is selected on the basis of the
A] length of the job
B] material of the job
C] diameter of the job
D] type of operation
77] Centre drilling is done at a
A] high spindle speed with a high feed
B] low spindle speed with a high feed
C] high spindle speed with a low feed
D] low spindle speed with a low feed

Measuring Instruments in Manufacturing Engineering

78] The least count of vernier caliper is
A] 0.01 mm

B] 0.02mm

C] 0.001 mm

D] 0.2 mm

vernier caliper

vernier caliper

Vernier Caliper

79] The graduations of a depth micrometer are...

A] Similar to an outside micrometer

B] In the reverse direction to that of the outside micrometer, both Thimble and sleeve

C] In the reverse direction only on the sleeve

D] In the direction only on the thimble

depth micrometer

depth micrometer

Depth Micrometer

80] The process of enlarging the end of a hole for accommodating the socket screw head is...

A] Reaming

B] Spot facing

C] Counter boring

D] Counter sinking

boring

Boring Operation

81]While choosing a boring tool for boring a given diameter, select

A] a long tool

B] a short tool

C] a long and stout tool

D] a short and stout tool

82] The cutting edge of the boring tool should be set for a small hole so that it is

A] 0.5 mm above the center

B] 0.5 mm below the center

C] 1 mm above the center

D] in the exact center

83] Bored holes are to be chamfered by using

A] a drill

B] triangular scraper

C] a cranked boring tool

D] a flat file

84] The tool used for boring deep holes is a

A] lathe mandrel

B] sleeve

C] drill

D] boring bar

E] auger bit

85] The cutting speed for rough boring is the

A] same as rough turning

B] same as drilling

C] same as knurling

D] same as thread cutting

86] The reamer is used for...

A] Drilling holes in thin sheets

B] Drilling deep holes

C] Removing burrs

D] Enlarging and finishing holes

reamer

reamer

Reamer

87] The reamer teeth are unevenly spaced because...
A] They are easy to manufacture
B] They can reduce chattering
C] They help to cut metal gradually
D] They help to remove the reamer easily
88] Which among the following is not a capability of reamers?
A] Finishing small holes
B] Finishing any machined profiles
C] Accuracy to closer limits
D] Producing high quality surface finish
89] The most important quality of any cutting fluid is
A] emulsification
B] specific heat
C] specific gravity
D] viscosity

cutting fluid 1

Cutting Fluid

90] By using coolants on workpieces we can choose

A] higher cutting speeds

B] lower cutting feeds

C] lower cutting speeds

D] heavy depth of cuts

91] The cutting speed for aluminium with H.S.S] tools is

A] 30 m/min

B] 50 m/min

C] 70 m/min

D] 130 m/min

92] The cutting speed for brass with a H.S.S] tool is

A] 10 m/min

B] 25 m/min

C] 70 m/min

D] 140 m/min

93] The distance, which the cutting edge of a tool passes over the material in a minute while machining is Know as...

A] RPM

B] Feed

C] Machine speed

D] Cutting speed

94] The cutting angle for chipping cast iron is...

A] 37.5°

B] 55°

C] 60°

D] 90°

95] The depth of cut is given by

A] the top slide
B] the cross-slide
C] the compound slide
D] adjusting the tool

96] For mounting a lathe chuck
A] start it by hand and then turn the power on
B] mount it on by power
C] mount it by hand
D] mount it with the help of a hammer

lathe chucks

lathe chuck

Lathe Four Jaw Chuck

97] The morse taper provided on drills used on lathe ranges between
A] MT1 to MT5
B] MT1 to MT4
C] MT0 to MT5
D] MT0 to MT4

98] Feeding the small drill too fast into the work may result in
A] breaking the drill
B] bending the drill

C] cutting an oval shape hole

D] increased production

99] Number of flutes in a twist drills are --------

A] 1

B] 2

C] 3

D] 4

100] Which one of the following drilling machines is used for drilling holes where electricity is not available?

A] Bench drilling machine

B] Pillar drilling machine

C] Redial drilling machine

D] Ratchet drilling machine

101] Which one of the following drilling machine is used for heavy duty work?

A] Bench drilling machine

B] Pillar drilling machine

C] Radial drilling machine

D] Electric hand drilling machine

102] The suitable cutting fluid for drilling mild steel in a lathe is

A] synthetic soluble oil

B] neat cutting oil

C] distilled water

D] soluble oil+water

103] The suitable cutting fluid for precision grinding is

A] Soluble oil

B] Synthetic soluble oil

C] Neat oil

D] Servo Cut's'

gringing wheel grinding wheel

Grinding Wheel

104] Advantage of using cutting fluid during grinding operation is ------

A] 5000 surface finish

B] Reduction in cutting forces

C] Reduction in hardening of the work piece

D] All of these]

105] Lubricant is necessary to ....]

A] run the machine smoothly taking least load

B] Run the machine quickly

C] Stop the machine immediately

D] Produce work piece of greater accuracy

106] The main purpose for using a lubricant in machine tools is to ------

A] Cool down the making parts

B] Prevent machine tool from heating

C] Wet the making parts for close contact

D] Minimize the friction between the making parts

107] Driving plates are used for

A] mounting fixtures and workpieces

B] driving shafts between Centre's with a lathe dog

C] facing operations only

D] internal operations only

108] Balancing is done in the face plate work

A] to increase the speed

B] to reduce the pressure on the tool

C] for uniform rotation of work

D] to get a good finish

109] A face plate is used to hold

A] a round job

B] a finished job

C] an irregular Job

D] a hollow job

110] Which is correct angle plate used with face plate

(A] Solid Type

(B] Box Type

(C] Adjustable Type

(D] None of them

angle plate

Angle Plate

111] Face plate is made from.....]

(A] Mild Steel

(B] Cast Iron

(C] Brass

(D] Aluminium

112] Which following accessories is use for odd an uneven job turning?

(A] Three Jaw Chuck

(B] Two Jaw Chuck

(C] Driving Plate

(D] Face Plate

113] An irregular shaped work piece is turned on a Lathe] Which one of the following work holding accessories is used?

A] Two Jaw chuck

B] Three Jaw chuck

C] Driving plate

D] Face plate

114]The pads of a steady rest are made of

A] carbon steel

B] lead

C] mild steel

D] brass

steady rest

Steady Rest

115] A steady rest is used
A] to hold jobs
B] for face plate work
C] to drive the job
D] to support the job
116] A follower steady is held on the
A] lathe bed
B] lathe carriage
C] lathe spindle
D] tailstock
117] When turning long work pieces, the following is used
A sleeve
B change gear
C steady rest
D bracket]
118] Knurling operation is done at the
A] turning spindle speed
B] high spindle speed
C] 1/3 of the turning spindle speed
D] 1/2 of the turning spindle speed

knurling tool

Knurling Tool

119] Knurling is the operation of

A] shearing

B] forming

C] turning

D] pressing

120] Mandrels are generally used when machining with

A] heavy cuts

B] short facing cuts

C] light cuts

D] boring tools

Limit Fit & Tolerances in Manufacturing Engineering

121] In the B.I.S system 25 hole deviations are specified by

A] small letters

B] small letters with numbers

C] small letters with tolerance

D] capital letters

122] The standard range of sizes covered in the B.I.S] system of limits and fits are

A] 0 to 10 mm

B] 0 to 100 mm

C] 25 to 400 mm

D] 0 to 500 mm

123] The basic size is the size

A] mentioned in the drawing

B] machined by the operator

C] based on which deviations are given

D] given by the instructor

124] Limits of size are

A] 2

B] 3

C] 4

D] 5

125] The number of fundamental deviations in the B.I.S] system are

A] 20

B] 22

C] 25

D] 28

126] The number of grade of tolerances in the B.I.S] system are

A] 12

B] 16

C] 18

D] 20

127] The size based on which the dimensional deviations are given is called...

A] Actual size

B] Basic size

C] Minimum limit of size

D] Maximum limit of Size

128] The size of parts made by .....] for provide interchange ability properties] (A] Measurement System

(B] Trial and Error System

(C] Limit and Tolerance System

(D] None of Them

129] Your job taper is correct if it is measured

A above the higher limit

B in between higher and lower limit

C below the lower limit]

130] When tolerance given in one side of the basic dimension, it is called --------

A].Tolerance system

B] Unilateral tolerance

C] Bilateral tolerance

D] Allowance System

131] A dimension is stated as (025 H7 in a drawing] The lower limit is -----------

A] 24.75 mm

B] 24.85 mm

C] 25.00 mm

D] 25-021 mm

132] The measured Size Of the dimensions of a component as called---------

A] Basic size

B] Nominal Size

C] Allowed size

D] Actual size

133] In the drawing the dimensions of a shaft is shown 40i 0068/0042, which is the size of Shaft within the tolerance?

A] 4.0.64 mm

B] 40.042 mm

C] 40.000 mm

D] 39.998 mm

134] In Hole basic system ----------

A] The size of the shaft is made constant

B] The Size of the hole is made constant

C] Only 'allowance is given on the hole

D] The permissible tolerance are given on the hole and the Shaft

135] The Size of a component is given as 24 -0.1] What does -O.1 indicates? _

A] Upper deviation is + 0.1 mm]

B] Lower deviation is 0.0 mm

C] Fundamental deviation is 0.0 mm

D] Lower deviation is _0.1 mm

136] The tolerance of a hole iS the difference between the -------

A] Maximum hole Size and maximum Shaft size

B] Maximum hole size and maximum hole Size

C] Minimum'hole size and maximum Shaft Size

D] Minimum hole Size and minimum shaft Size

137] A hole whose lower deviation is zero is called basic hole] Which one of the following letter indicates basic hole?]

A] E

B] F

C] G'

D] H

138] Which one having upper deviation zero?

A] Bassc Shaft

B] Basic hole

C] Tolerance

D] Clearance

139] A ball bearing on a shaft is type of fit? ,

A] Clearance fit

B] Driving fit

C] Shrinkage fit

D] None of the above

140] Which one of the following is important factor required to achieve the interchange ability in mass production?]

A] Geometrical accuracy]

B] Standardization

C] Dimensional accuracy

D] Surface finish

141] In the BIS system of limits and fits, the grade of tolerance are represented by number Symbols and there are ---------i

A] 14 grades of tolerance

B] 16 grades of tolerance

C] 18 grades of tolerance ‘

D] 20 grades of tolerance

142] A Product is said to have the quality when ....]

A] Its shape and dimensions are within the limit

B] It is fit for use

C] It appears to be very good

D] The choice of material is right

143] The maximum clearance required between hole’30 +0.021, 0.000 and shaft 30 -0.110, 0.143 is.

A] 0.110 mm ‘

B]0.131 mm

C] 0.164 mm

D] 0.143 mm

144] A dimension is stated as 25 .1002 mm in a drawing] What is the tolerance?

A] +0.02 mm’

B] +0.04 mm

C] -0.02 mm

D] 25.00 mm

145] A pin is fitted in a hole] The tolerance zone of the pin is entirely above that of hole] The fit obtained will be?

A] Clearance fit

B] Transition fit

C] Interference fit

D] Running fit

146] Interchange ability is normally applied for? _

A] Repairing of parts

B] Mass production

C] Single piece production

D] All of these

147] Tolerance is given to the part size to...........]

A] Production the part within the required permissible size error

B] Increase the production

C] Decrease the Production

D] Finish the components approximately

148] Which one of the following is the clearance fit under the whole basic system?

A] 20 H7/p6‘

B] 2067/211

C] ZOG/gll]

D] 20H/g11]

149] The three classes of fits as per BIS system aré ....] ~]

A] Clearance fit, interference fit and transition fit

B] Medium fit, push fit and tight fit

C] Flat fit, round fit and square fit

D] ‘Sliding fit ’, loose fit and shrinkage fit

150] Which one of the following tolerance specifications has a maximum dimensionless than 20 mm?

A] 20 +0.2,-0.3

B] 20 320.2

C] 20 -0.2, 0.3 e

D]m 20 +500, ~03

151] Difference between the maximum and minimum limit is -~-~~~~-~~~~~ ‘

A] Single informant

B] Basic shaft

C] Clearance
D] Tolerance
152] A shaft 55 running freely in bush bearing the type of fit is ---------
A] Clearance fit
B] Driving plate
C] shrinkage fit
D] None of the above
153] The taper ratio of the morse taper is
A] 1 in 10
B] 1 in 15
C] 1 in 20
D] 1 in 25
154] The morse standard taper is available in
A] 16 Nos
B] 12 Nos
C] 10 Nos
D] 8 Nos
155] Taper turning by offsetting the tailstock method can produce
A] an internal taper
B] an internal taper thread
C] an external taper
D] both external and internal tapers

taper turning attachment

taper turning

Taper by Tailstock Offset

156] By using the taper turning attachment, tapers can be turned with a setting angle up to
A] 10°
B] 15°

C] 20◦

D] 30◦

157] The accuracy of a taper is generally checked by means of......

A] taper gauges

B] gauge blocks

C] indicator and height gauge

D] 'V' blocks

158] Turning tapers by the compound rest method involves working solely with

Decimal measurements

B fractional measurements

C metric measurements

D angular measurements]

159] Long tapers are produced

A with the taper turning attachment

B with the compound slide

C by setting over the tail stock

D by adjusting the cross slide]

160] The length of turned tapers are checked with

A vernier calliper

B micrometer

C inside callper

D dial test indicator]

161] The disadvantages of taper turning using the com] pound slide are

A] only long tapers can be turned

B] only very large tapers can be turned

C] only manual in feed is possible

D] only short tapers can be turned due to the restrictions of the compound slide]

162] External tapers are checked with

A] limit plug gauge

B] taper ring gauge

C]taper plug gauge

D] thread plug gauge]

163] The use of a taper turned on lathe is ----

A] Assist to transmit drive in the assembled parts

B] Used for Assembly and disassembly of parts

C] Give self alignment in the assembled parts

164] Which type of method is used in mass production of production of producing small length of taper?

A] Form tool

B] Compound slide

C] Tailstock offset.

D] Taper turning attachment

165] Morse standard taper is one of the internationally accepted standards taper, which is available in numbers from--------

A]1to7

B]1 to 8

C] O to 7

D] 0 to 8

166] Which taper turning method is used for cutting steep taper?

A] Set over method

B] Taper turning attachment

C] Form tool

D] Swivelling the compound rest

167] Morse taper is used in which of the following machine components -...

A] Spindles of lathe

B] Spindles of drill machine

C] Shanks of reamers

D] All of these

168] For mass production of the taper which one of the following method is used.......]

A] Tailstock offset method

B] Taper turning attachment method

C] Form too method

D] Compound slide method

169] The major diameter of the taper is 40 mm, minor diameter is 30 mm] The total length of the job is 100 mm is tapered then offset is given by -

A] 5 mm

B] 7.5 mm

C] 12 mm

D] 9 mm

170] The accuracy of an ordinary bevel protractor is --' ------------degree]

A] One

B] Three

C] Two

D] Four

171] The least count of a vernier bevel protractor is...

A] 1”

B] 5’

C] 1◦

D] 5 ◦

172] The part of a vernier bevel protractor which is normally used as a reference base for measuring angles is the...

A] Blade

B] Stock

C] Disc

C] Main scale

173] The part of a vernier bevel protector on which main scale divisions are marked is the...

A] Stock

B] Dial

C] Disc

D] Adjustable blade

174] The part of a bevel protractor, which comes in contact with the inclined surface while measuring is the...

A] Blade

B] Stock

C] Disc

D] Dial

175] The value of each division of the main scale of a vernier bevel protractor is...

A] 5’

B] 1◦

C] 5◦

D.10◦

176] The value of each division of the vernier scale of a bevel protractor is...

A] 1◦

B] 1◦5’

C] 1◦55’

D.5'

177] The part of the vernier bevel protractor on which main scale divisions are marked

A stock

B dial

C disc

D adjustable blade

178] In Vernier bevel protractor is designed to measure?

A] Acute angles

B] Obtuse angles

C] Acute and Obtuse angle

D] Liner dimensions

179] To get least count of 5 in a vernier bevel protractor the 23° main scale are divided into -..

A] 12 equal parts on vernier scale

B] 22 equal parts on vernier scale

C] 24 equal parts on vernier scale

D] 25 equal parts on vernier scale

180] Which of the following is not the part of a combination set?

A] Stock

B] Square head

C] Protractor head

D] Centre head

181] The datum, form which the measurements of the vernier height gauge are taken, is...

A] The beam

B] The vernier slide

C] The base

D] Above the scriber poing

vernier height gauge vernier height guage

Vernier Height Gauge

182]The part of a vernier height gauge on which the main scale divisions are graduated is the...

A] Base

B] Beam

C] Fine setting device

D] The vernier plate

183] On which part of the vernier height gauge are the main scale division graduated?]

A] Base

B] Vernier plate

C] Beam

D] Fine adjusting unit

184] For marking purpose a Vernier height gauge must be on the --------

A] Bed of a machine tool

B] Surface plate

C] Square block

D] Any flat surface

185] Before using Vernier height gauge make sure that the --------

A] Locking screw is in a locked position

B] Scriber is Locked

C] Zero of the vernier coincides with zero of the main scale

D] Gib is Provided

186] The least count Of a vernier height gauge is...........]

A] 0.05 mm

B] 0.1 mm

C] 0.02 mm

D] 0001 mm

187] Which laying out the vernier height gauge must be used on the ----------

A] V block

B] Machine bed

C] Surface plate

D] Any flat surface

188] The part which is slides on the beam of a vernier height gauge is known as a ------

A] Base

B] Beam scale

C] Scriber

D] Vernier slide

189] The base of the vernier height gauge is generally made out of ---------

A] Cast iron]

B] Steel

C] Aluminium alloy

D] Tungsten carbide

190] Which instrument iis used for marking layout?

A] Micrometer

B] Vernier

C] Depth gauge

D] Vernier height gauge

191] While marking with a Vernier height gauge, the work piece is generally ----------

A] Supported by an angle plate

B] Supported by another work piece

C] Held by one hand

D] Held without support

192] Which of the following is not the part of a combination set?

A] Stock

B] Square head

C] Protractor head

D] Centre head

Engineering Drawing in Manufacturing Engineering

18]The 'T' square is used for drawing lines ......

a] inclined

b] curved

c] vertical
d] horizontal
19] For drawing large size circle is drawn by.....
a] straight bar
b] lengthening bar
c] big bar
d] small bar
20] To draw or measure angle is used by.....
a]set square
b] protractor
c] 'T' square
d] none of these
21] The grade of pencil is used to sketching lettering ....
a] conical point
b] chisel point
c] soft
d] low
22] For drawing thin lines of uniform thickness the pencil should be sharpened in the form of ....
a] chisel edge
b]conical
c] pointed
d] none of these
23] What is used for drawing curves which can not drawn by compass
a] small compass
b] French curve
c] protractor
d] none of these
24]Unnecessary lines is removed by .....
a] Duster
b] sand paper block
c] eraser
d] none of these
25] Circle and arcs are drawn by means of .....l.
a] compass
b] divider
c] lengthening bar
d]none of these

26] Inking pen is used in drawing ......
a] horizontal line
b] non circular arcs
c] vertical lines
d] <u>all of these</u>
27] The card board scale are available in set of .....
a] 7
b] <u>8</u>
c] 6
d] 9
28] The convenient length size of 30 -60°-90° set square for used in school and colleges are......
a] 250
b] 200
c] 300
d] none of these
29] Drawing board is shape of ....
a] square
b] <u>rectangular</u>
c] triangular
d] none of these
30] The 'T' square , set square ,scale protractor are complain use in.......
a] protractor
b] <u>mini drafter</u>
c] set square
d] none of these
31]Set square , T square edges are bevelled for the purpose of....
a] curve line
b] <u>inking lines</u>
b] taking measurements
d] none of these
32]Geometrical construction which are mostly based on plane geometry and which are very.......
a] Accuracy
b] Quality
c] <u>Essential</u>
d] Superior quality
33] How much method of drawing the regular polygons.......

a] Inscribe circle method and arc method
b] General method for drawing any polygon
c] Alternative method
d] <u>All of these</u>

34] The line AB can be divided into .... equal parts.
a] <u>7</u>
b] 10
c] 15
d] All of them

35] Which method of constructing triangl in circle......
a] <u>Inscribing</u>
b] Describing
c] Both a and b
d] None of these

36] When two sides of the hexagon are required to be horizontal the starting point for stepping equal division should be on an end of the.....
a] <u>Horizontal diameter</u>
b] Vertical diameter
c] Inclined diameter
d] None of these

37] If two sides of hexagon are required to be vertical the starting point should be on an end of the....
a] Inclined diameter
b] Horizontal diameter
c] <u>Vertical diameter</u>
d] None of these

38] The section obtained by the inter section of the right circular cone by a plane in different position relative to the axis of the cone are called.......
a] <u>Conics</u>
b] Circles
c] Triangles
d] Half circle

39] When the section plane is inclined to the axis and cuts all the generators on one side on a apex the section is in......
a] Conic section
b] <u>Ellipse</u>
c] Parabola
d] Hyperbola

40] When the section plane is inclined to the axis and is parallel to one of the generators the section is a ....

a] Ellipse

b] Parabola

c] Hyperbola

d] Cycloid

41] Use of elliptical curve is........

a] Arches

b] Dams and monuments

c] Manholes, gland & stuffing boxes

d] All of these

42] Use of parabolic curve is.........

a] Bridges & arches

b] Sound reflectors

c] Light reflectors

d] All of these

43] Use of hyperbolical curve is......

a] Cooling towers and water channel

b] Dames

c] Bridges

d] All of these

44] When the point is within the circle, the curve is called an.......

a] Superior trochoid

b] Interior trochoid

c] Trochoid

d] Isotrochoid

45] When the point outside the circle then the curve is called as......

a] Interior trochoid

b] Superior trochoid

c] Trochoid

d] Insuperior trochoid

46] The curve general by a point on a circumference of a circle, which rolls without slipping along another circle it is called.......

a] Epicycloids

b] Hypocycloid

c] Involute

d] None of these

47] When the circle rolls inside another circle the curve is called.......

a] Hypocycloid
b] Epicycloids
c] Trochoid
d] Hypotrochoid
48] The use of archemedian spiral curve is made in........
a] Teeth profiles of helical gears
b] Profiles of cams
c] Both a & b
d] None of these
49] The cams are widely used in........
a] Automates
b] Printing machines
c] C engines
d] All of these
50] Spring index =
a] Diameter of coil / diameter of a wire
b] Diameter of wire /diameter of coil
c] Mean diameter of wire / diameter of coil
d] Mean diameter of a coil / diameter of wire
51] Eccentricity =
a] Distance of a point from the focus / distance of the point from directrix
b] Distance of focus from point / distance of point from
c] Distance of point from focus / distance of directrix of point
d] Distance of point from directrix / distance of point from focus
52] Mathematically an ellipse can be described by equation.....
a] $a^2 / X^2 + y^2 / b^2 = 1$
b] $x^2 / a^2 + y^2 / b^2$
c] $x^2 / a^2 + y^2 / b^2 = 0$
d] $x^2 / a^2 + y^2 / b^2 = 1$
53] Mathematically a parabola can be described by an equation......
a] $y^2 = 4ax$
b] $x^2 = 2ay$
c] $x^2 = 4ay$
d] Both a & b
54] Mathematically hyperbola can be described by an equation.......
a] $x^2 /a^2 - y^2 /b^2 = 1$
b] $x^2 /y^2 - y^2 /x^2 = 0$

c] Both a & b

d] None of these

55] Cycloid can be described by an equation......

a] y = a(1-cos Ø]

b] x = a(Ø -sin Ø]

c] Both a & b

d] None of these

56] The mathematically represented hypocycloid is.....

a] Y = a $\cos^3$ Ø, X = a $\sin^3$ Ø

b] X = a $\sin^3$ Ø, Y = a $\cos^3$ Ø

c] X = a $\cos^3$ Ø, Y = a $\sin^3$ Ø

d] None of these

57] Mathematically represented by involute is

a] X = r sin Ø - r Ø cos Ø, Y = r cos + r Ø sin Ø

b] X = r sin Ø + r cos Ø, Y = r cos Ø – r Ø sin Ø

c] Y = r Ø cos Ø – r sin Ø, X = r sin Ø – r Ø cos Ø

d] X = r cos Ø + r Ø sin Ø, Y =r sin Ø - r Ø cos Ø

58] The lines from the object to the plane are called.......

a] Projection

b] Projector

c] Reference plane

d] None of these

59] The orthographic projection an object is represented by View on the mutual perpendicular projection lines

a] Two or three

b] Three or two

c] Three or four

d] None of these

60] When the projectors are parallel to each other & also perpendicular to the plane, the projection is called......

a] Isometric projection

b] Oblique projection

c] Orthographic projection

d] Perspective projection

61] The two planes employed for the purpose of Orthographic projections are......

a] Auxillary plane

d] Horizontal plane

c] Reference plane

d] None of these

62] The line in which they intersect is termed the reference line & is denoted by the letters.......

a] AB

b] YZ

c] XY

d] None of these

63] The projection on the VP is called........

a] Side view

b] Front view

c] Top view

d] All of these

64] ....Method, when the views are drawn in their relative positions, the plane comes below the elevation. The view of the object as observed from the left-side the right of elevation.

a] Plane of projection

b] First angle projection

c] Third angle projection

d] None of these

65] Third angle projection method, the object is assumed to be situated in the........ quadrant.

a] First quadrant

b] Second quadrant

c] Third quadrant

d] Fourth quadrant

66] .... Method of projection is used in U.S.A & also in other countries.

a] plane of projection

b] Orthographic projection

c] First-angle projection

d] Third angle projection

67] When an object is situated on the ground, in first angle projection method, the bottom of its ..... will co-inside with XY

a] Top view

b] Front view

c] side view

d] All of these

68] The important element of this projection system

a] An object

b] Plane of projection

c] An observer

d] All of these

69] When line AB is parallel to HP hence ....

a] It' front view to AB

b] It''s side view equal to AB

c] It's top view equal to AB

d] None of these

70] When a line is parallel to a plane; it's projection on plane is equal to it's ;

a] True length

b] True shape

c] True size

d] None of these

71] The point is parallel in which the line or line produced meet the point is plane is called it's ....

a] Line

b] ratio

c] Trace

d] none of these

72] .... is the shortest distance between two points.

a] a line

b] a point

c] a straight line

d] none of these

73] When the line intersect horizontal plane that's called.....

a] horizontal trace

b] vertical trace

c] trace of line

d] none of these

74]Planes may be divided into two main types ......

a] Perpendicular planes, auxillary planes

b] Perpendicular plane, oblique planes

c] Auxillary planes , perpendicular planes

d] none of these

75] Planes which are inclined to the reference plane are called......

a] Auxillary plane

b] obliqeu plane

c] Perpendicular planes

d] picture plane

76] When a plane is perpendicular to a reference plane it's projection on that plane is a..........

a] horizontal line

b] parallel line

c] straight line

d] none of these

77] When a plane is parallel to a reference plane , it's projection on that plane shows........

a] It's true shape &size

b] It's true length & size

c] It's true height & size

d] none of these

78] Plane perpendicular to VP & HP that plane is called as ....

a] Auxillary Plane

b] Oblique Plane

c] Perpendicular Plane

d] None of these

79] Perpendicular plane can be divides into the following types.........

a] Perpendicular to both the reference planes.

b] Perpendicular to one plane & parallel to other

c] Perpendicular to one plane & inclined to other

d] All of these

80] The planes have only two dimensions, viz........

a] Length & breadth

b] Length & height

c] Length & thickness

d] All of these

81] The imaginary line of prism joining the centrs of the bases called.........

a] Faces

b] Axis

c] Apex

d] Base

82] A right & regular prism has it's axis....... to the bases

a] Parallel
b] Perpendicular
c] Inclined
d] None of these

83] When a pyramid or a cone is cut by a plane parallel to it's base thus removing the top portion, the remaining portion is called it's.........
a] Sphere
b] Cone
c] Cylinder
d] Frustum

84] Oblique cylinder & cones have their axes........ to their base
a] Inclined
b] Parallel
c] Perpendicular
d] All of these

85] Projection of two equal sphere s resting on the ground & in contact with each other, with the line joining there centre parallel to the..........
a] A VP
b] VP
c] HP
d] All of these

86] Projections of section on the other plane to which it is inclined is called.......
a] Section planes
b] Apparent section
c] True shape of sphere
d] None of these

87] When the section plane is parallel to the HP or the ground, the true shape of the section will be seen in.........
a] Front view
b] Side view
c] Top view
d] All of these

88] Surface of solid are laid out on a plane the figure obtained is called its........
a] Interpenetration
b] Development
c] Intersection

d] None of these

89] Development of surfaces is essential in.........

a] Foundry shop

b] <u>Sheet metal work</u>

c] Fitting shop

d] None of these

90] Which method of development used in transition pieces?

a] Parallel diameter

b] Radial line method

c] <u>Triangulation method</u>

d] Approximate method

91] Which method of development used in pyramids and cones.........

a] <u>Radial line method</u>

b] Parallel line method

c] Approximate method

d] Triangulation method

92] Parallel line method is used in..........

a] Prism

b] Cylinder

c] Cubes

d] <u>All of these</u>

93] Which method of development used in surface as sphere, paraboloid, ellipsoid, hyperboloid, and helicoids

a] Radial line method

b] Triangulation method

c] <u>Approximate method</u>

d] Parallel line method

94] Zone method and lune method is used in development of........

a] Prisms

b] Cones

c] <u>Sphere</u>

d] Pyramids

95] Calculation the subtended angle Θ by the formula $\Theta = 360^0 \times$ radius of the base circle

a] <u>Length of axis</u>

b] <u>Slant height</u>

c] Radius of axis

d] None of these

96] In engineering practice, objects constructed may have constituent part, the surfaces of which intersect one another in lines called........ of intersection.

a] Lines
b] Cones
c] Cylinder
d] Prisms

97] The line of interaction may be depending upon the nature of.......

a] Intersection surface
b] Intersecting solids
c] Intersection cones
d] None of these

98] The two plane surface intersect in a........ line

a] Curve
b] Straight
c] Plane
d] All of these

99] The line of intersection between two curved surface or between......... Surface and a curved surface is a curve.

a] A curved
b] A plane
c] A solids
d] None of these

100] When a solids completely penetration another solids there will be two lines of intersection. These lines are sometimes called the line or........

a] Line of interpenetration
b] Curve of interpenetration
c] Solids of interpenetration
d] All of these

101] Use of penetration curve is.......

a] Sheet metal work
b] Fitting shop
c] Fabricating work
d] Foundry shop

102] Methods of determining the line of intersection between surface of two interpenetration.........

a] Approximate method & radial line method
b] Line method and cutting plane method

c] Triangulation method and parallel line method
d] None of these
103] Example of interpenetration is..........
a] Two prism intersection
b] Cylinder and prism intersection
c] Cone and cylinders intersection
d] All of these
104] Two cylinder intersection is example of.........
a] Intersection
b] Interpenetration
c] Cone intersection
d] None of these
105] .... Method is explained in detail while solving illustrative problems
a] Line method
b] Radial line method
c] Cutting plane method
d] Parallel line method
106] What is a type of isometric projection?
a] Pictorial projection
b] Orthographic projection
c] Perspective projection
d] Oblique Projection
107] Isometric views have been drawn........
a] Full scale
b] Half scale
c] True length
d] True scale
108] The line parallel to isometric axis are called........
a] Isometric axis
b] Isometric line
c] Isometric planes
d] Isometric views
109] The isometric projection is reduce in the ratio.........
a] 3 :
b] 1 : 2
c] 2 : 2
d] 2 : 3

110] The isometric projection of circle drawn with........

a] Isometric Plane

b] Isometric graph

c] Isometric Drawing

d] <u>Isometric Scale</u>

111] The major axis of the ellipse is long than...............

a] Radius of the circle

b] True diameter

c] <u>Diameter of the circle</u>

d] None of these

112] Makes practice for drawing of isometric view using........

a] Isometric planes

b] Isometric lines

c] <u>Isometric graph</u>

d] Isometric view

113] Use of parabolic curve is

a] <u>Sound reflectors</u>

b] Dams

c] Man hole of boiler

d] Gland & stuffing box

114] When the section plane is inclined the true shape of section on

a] AVP

b] VP

c] HP

d] <u>A/P</u>

115] When section plane is perpendicular to both the HP & VP the true shape of section on

a]Top view

b] <u>Side view</u>

c] Front view

d]None of this

116] When view projected on auxiliary planes are called

a] <u>Auxiliary view</u>

b Sectiona! view

c] Front view

d] None of these

117] Invisible features of an object are shown by means of

a] Outline

b] Chain lines

c] Hidden lines

d] None of these

118] Importance of sectional view on drawing for

a] Internal details

b] Outer details

c] Hatching

d] None of these

119] The component is cut by a straight cutting plane is divided in to two parts

a] Half section

b] Full section

c] Offset section

d] Removed section

120] section line is two different parts (pieces] in contact should be drown in...

a] Same direction

b] Opposite direction

c]parallel direction

d] None of these

121] When area to be sectioned in very small as for this plate and structural members blacked in section may be used. A space of not less than

a] 0.07mm

b] 0.7mm

c] 0.05mm

d] 0.5mm

122] The sum of interior angles of polygon is equal

a] (2*n-4]*Right angle

b] (2*n]*Right angle-4

c] (2*4-n]*Right angle

d] (2-4*n]*Right angle

123] One micron is equal to ....mm

a] 0.001

b] 1000

c] 0.01

d] 0.1

124] Development of surface is essential in.....

a] foundry shop

b] sheet metal work
c] fitting shop
d] none of these

125] Which method of development used in transition piece?
a] parallel line method
b] radial line method
c] triangulation method
d] none of these

126] The isometric projection is reduced in the ratio of
a] √2:√3
b] √3:√2
c] 1:√2
d] none of these

127] When measurements are required in three units the scale is used....
a] full scale
b] plain scale
c] half scale
d] none of these

128]Isometric drawing is larger in production about isometric projection is....
a] 22.5%
b] 0.815
c] 9/11
d] none of these

129] While isometric of sphere of spherical parts.......is must be used.
a] full scale
b] isometric length
c] true length
d] half scale

130] When circle draw with isometric scale the length of major axis of the ellipse to the ....
a] true diameter
b] isometric diameter
c] isometric diameter
d] none of these

131] In isometric view which contain a large number of non –isometric lines which method is used
a] box method

b] off-set method

c] <u>co-ordinate method</u>

d] centre lay out method

132] When drawing is drawn smaller than actual size of object .....

a] full scale

b] enlarging scale

c] <u>reducing scale</u>

d] none of these

133] When e=1 curve is called.....

a] <u>parabola</u>

b] hyperbola

c] ellipse

d] none of these

134]Compare with isometric drawing the advantage of oblique projection is....

a] <u>front face is in true shape</u>

b] two axis are always perpendicular to each othe

c] receding axis is taken at some convenient angles

d] none of these

135]If all the receding edges are drawn true length the oblique projection is called...

a] <u>cavilier projection</u>

b] cabinet projection

c] general projection

d] none of these

136] The large object such as building the point is usually taken height of .....

a] 0.8mm

b] 1.2mm

c] <u>1.8mm</u>

d] 1.5mm

137] Central plane is the imaginary vertical plane which passes through....

a] <u>P. P</u>

b] H.L

c] G.P

d] C.P

138] When object is parallel to P.P the perspective is called......

a] one point
b] two point
c] three point
d] none of these

139] The line drawn through the station point from the picture plane shall be ....

a] P.A
b] H.L
c] G.L
d] C

140] The distance of the station point from the picture plane shall be .....

a] Max. Diameter of the object
b] Twice the max. Diameter of the object
c] Half the max. Diameter of the object
d] none of these

141] In isometric view of hexagonal plane all the sides of hexagon is .....

a] equal length
b] unequal length
c] none of these

142] When all the faces are equal & regular the polyhedron is said....

a] regular
b] prisms
c] irregular
d] pyramid

143] Oblique prisms &pyramid have ......

a] axis perpendicular to the base
b] axis inclined to the base
c] faces inclined to the H.P
d] none of these

144] Icosahedrons has equal equilateral triangular faces

a] 12
b] 8
c] 20
d] 6

145] When a pyramid or cone is cut by a plane parallel to its base is called.....

a] pyramid
b] turned carted

c] frustum

d] none of these

146] Plane which are inclined to both the reference plane is called ......

a] oblique plane

b] perpendicular plane

c] inclined plane

d] none of these

147] When a line parallel to H.P & perpendicular to V.P the trace line is.....

a] V.T

b] H.T

c] no trace

d] V.T& H.T

148] When a line parallel to the V.P and inclined to H.P the true length of line in.....

a] front view

b] top view

c] side view

d] none of these

149] When point situated in front quadrant

a] above the H.P & in front of V.P

b] below the H.P & in front of V.P

c] behind the V.P & above H.P

d] below the H.P & behind the V.P

150] Find the quadrant of point "b" is 15 mm above H.P and 25mm behind the V.P

a] I st

b] III rd

c] IIII th

d] II nd

151] In first angle projection front view is ......

a] above the top view

b] below the top view

c] above the side view

d] below the side view

152] In orthographic projection the projectors are ....

a] parallel to plane

b] perpendicular to plane

c] inclined to plane

d] none of these

153] L.H.S.V means.........

a] length of side view

b] left hand view

c] right hand view

d] left hand side view

154] The object lines between the observer and the plane of projection is ....

a] 3rd angle

b] 1st angle

c] 4th angle

d] 2nd angle

155] In third angle projection plane of projection is assumed to be ......

a] non transparent

b] quadrant

c] transparent

d] dihedral angle

156] In third angle projection top view is always on......

a] above front view

b] above top view

c] below the front view

d] below the side view

157] Four quadrants which may be called as......

a] anticlockwise

b] first and third angle

c] dihedral angles

d] none of these

158] In first angle projection method the view see from the left is placed on .....

a] left of the front view

b] right of front view

c] above the top view

d] below the front view

159] The size of A2 paper is .....

a] 297*420

b] 594*841

c] 420*594

d] 210*297

160] The edge of board on which 'T' square is sli9ding is called ......

a] straight edge

b] working edge

c] chisel edge

d] none of these

161] The size of title block as recommended by B.I.S . is .....

a] 185*65

b] 150*50

c] 170*65

d] none of these

162] For A2 size sheet the number of zones suggested by B.I.S. along the length & width.......

a] 12,8

b] 16,12

c] 8,6

d] none of these

163] The drawing sheet is so folded that...... is always on the top.

a] drawing

b] lettering

c] title block

d] none of these

164] In free hand sketching horizontal lines are sketched from.......

a] right to left

b] up to down

c] left to right

d] none of these

165] When drawing is down smaller than actual size of object

a] enlarging scale

b] reducing scale

c] full scale

d] none of these

166] The ratio of the length of the object represented on drawing to the actual length of object is called.......

a] full scale

b] R.F.

c] half scale

d] plain scale

167] When measurements are required in three unit the scale is used.....
a] full scale
b] half scale
c] plain scale
d] none of these

168] When protractor is not available the scale of chord is used ......
a] measure length
b] measure angle
c] measure scale
d] none of these

169] The least count of a vernier calliper is ....
a] 0.001
b] <u>0.02</u>
c] 0.001
d] 0.0002

170] Which scale is used to read a very small unit with great accuracy?
a] plain scale
b] <u>diagonal scale</u>
c] scale of chord
d] vernier scale

171] The R.F. is greater than one (1] the scale is ....
a] plain scale
b] diagonal scale
c] <u>enlarging scale</u>
d] reducing scale

AutoCAD for Manufacturing Engineering

1] Which is the latest version of AutoCAD software?
a) 2016
b) 2017
c) <u>2018</u>
d) 2019

2] Which key is used to obtain properties palette in AutoCAD?
a) <u>Control+1</u>
b) Control+2
c) Control+3
d) Control+4

3] AutoCAD was first released in the year:
a) 1858

b) 1966
c) 1898
d) 1982

4] How many units are available in AutoCAD?

a) 4
b) 5
c) 7
d) 6

5] Which mode allows the user to draw 90° straight lines :

a) Osnap
b) Ortho
c) Linear
d) Polar tracking

6] To obtain parallel lines, concentric circles and parallel curves; __________ is used.

a) Array
b) Fillet
c) Copy
d) Offset

7] The default grid spacing in both X and Y directions is:

a) 10
b) 20
c) 5
d) 15

8] How many workspaces are available in AutoCAD?

a) 2
b) 4
c) 3
d) 5

9] Scale command can be accessed easily by typing:

a) SL
b) S
c) SC
d) C

10] Which command is used to divide the object into segments having predefined length?

a) Divide
b) Chamfer

c) Trim

d) Measure

11] How many grip points does a circle have?

a) 5

b) 4

c) 3

d) 2

] When drawing in 2D, what axis do you NOT work with?

A] X

B] Y

C] Z

D] WCS

] The primary difference between the Model tab and the Layout tab(s) is _____.

A] the Model tab is used for drawing in 3D and a Layout is used for drawing in 2D

B] the Model tab is where you create the drawing and a Layout tab represents the sheet that you will plot or print on

C] the color of the background

D] the Model tab displays the drawing you are copying from and the Layout tab is where you lay out the new drawing

] Which of the following is NOT a property of an object

A] Line weight

B] Measure

C] Hyperlink

D] Elevation

] Which command convert discrete objects in polyline

A] Union

B] Subtract

C] Join

D] Polyline

] To print the entire project, you will choose to regulate what to plot

A] Display

B] Extends

C] Limits

D] Window

] What is the usefulness of viewports

A] Allows us to see the screen or on paper different views of the same project

B] Give us the ability to see projects have become a newer version of AutoCAD from our

C] We can make a change in one part of the plan, without affecting the rest

D] None of the above

] What is the difference between the Scale command from the command Zoom

A] Scale for single object, while the Zoom whole plan

B] No difference

C] H Scale can grow / shrink a shape up 10 times, while the Zoom has no limits

D] H Scale changes the size of objects, while the Zoom changes the visibility of the project

] When to fix a block attribute

A] Before you fix the block

B] When I make the block

C] After fix the block

D] No matter the number

] What you cannot create from the command Offset

A] Vertical straight

B] Concentric circles

C] Three parallel lines

D] Parallel arcs

] By what symbol shows the snap point to the closest point

A] with circles and dots in the center

B] With two triangle

C] With three orthogonal

D] With Diamond

] Which state grid is use to design perspective

A] Parametric

B] Isometric

C] Pro-optic

D] Rectangular

] If I want to draw a line in the direction 07:30 (local time) will give an angle

A] -135 degrees

B] 270 degrees
C] -225 degrees
D] None of the above

] When in absolute Cartesian coordinates have points A (10.8) and B (6.5), then to make a line from A -> B with relative polar coordinates will write

A] @ -5 <36.88
B] @ 4 <30
C] @ 5 <216.88
D] @ 3 <60

] What is the minimum allowable number of layers in a drawing

A] 0
B] 5
C] 1
D] 2

] Which of the following is not a keyboard shortcut of AutoCAD?

A] Ctrl + P
B] Alt + F4
C] Ctrl + F4
D] Alt + B

] Why do we have 16,7 M colors in RGB

A] Because so one can distinguish man
B] since this is the limit of graphics cards
C] For each color we have 256 shades and colors combination third
D] Because we want compatibility between PC and Macintosh

] What setting gradient allows us to fill an open area?

A] Gap
B] Tolerance
C] Transparency
D] Open

] What are the various options from left to right and the opposite direction?

A] Choose a different category of objects
B] select objects according to their color
C] Select objects according to their position
D] No difference

] Which is corresponded to zoom mouse wheel?

A] Zoom in / zoom out

B] pan & scan
C] extents / all
D] scale
] What command allows us to select objects based on some status?
A] Properties
B] Qselect
C] Pselect
D] Attributes
] How to make a random line with an angle of 40 degrees to the x axis
A] will write 0 <40
B] will write 2 <40
C] will write 3<40
D] will write 4 <40
] Which of the following file extensions cannot open the AutoCAD
A] dwg
B] dxf
C] dot
D] dws
] A surveyor with a headband to measure the dimensions of a site, he make measurements by
A] No one method
B] Related Cartesian coordinates
C] Absolute polar coordinates
D] None of the above
] What is the command used for Plagiostomi angle?
A] Chamfer
B] Fillet
C] Offset
D] Mirror
] When should I use the Block Editor
A] To write text block
B] To fix outer block
C] To fix dynamic block
D] To store it in another version of AutoCAD
] If the scheme that stores will be opened in AutoCAD 2006 then you must save it in
A] AutoCAD 2004 dwg
B] AutoCAD 2006 dwg

C] AutoCAD 2007 dwg
D] None of the above
] Print scale 1:50 means that
A] The draft is 50 times less expensive than the original
B] A 3 cm corresponds to half a meter
C] A measure corresponds to 50 cm
D] None of the above
29] What do the letters UCS
A] Uniform Calculator System
B] United CAD System
C] Universal CAD Settings
D] Universal Coordinate System

] What is the difference of two regular 8-gonon, which is one inscribed and another circumscribed circle
A] No difference
B] different opening angles
C] different side length
D] different crowd sides

] If during the CCW measurement result gives an angle 135 degrees, the same CW angle measured is
A] 225 degrees
B] -135 degrees
C] -225 degrees
D] 135 degrees

] What does associative hatch
A] Monitors the changes in shape that fills
B] Relates to the other hatch plan
C] Both of the above
D] None of the above

] What is the difference between command Plot and Print
A] plot command prints only big plans
B] The plot command for CNC (CAM)
C] No difference
D] print command can print up to A3 size paper

] If you change the scale list a project that I have started from 1:50 1:10 then

A] You will have to start over

B] You should not raise the objects already exist (scale) by 5

C] You will not need to change anything in hitherto methodology

D] should be converted into new items that will add based on the new scale

] Which of the following is NOT a unit of length measurement?

A] Yards

B] Parsecs

C] Microns

D] Grads

] What does the command Wblock

A] Warp-speed block

B] Write block

C] Window block

D] Wide-area block

] Where should you pay attention when you are working with autocad commands?

A] Drawing area

B] Status bar

C] Tool bars

D] Command window

] Polar coordinates are used mostly for drawing______

A] Arc

B] Ellipse

C] Angular lines

D] None of the above

] How many SNAP points does an object have?

A] 1

B] 4

C] 5

D] Depend on object

] How many points do you need to define for the rectangle command?

A] One

B] Two

C] Three

D] Four

] How many AutoCAD objects are in a rectangle?

A] One

B] Two

C] Three

D] Four

] How will you deselect an object while you are selecting set of objects?

A] Ctrl+ click on the object to be removed

B] Shift + Click on the object to be removed

C] Alt + Click on the object to be removed

D] None of the above

] How long will a line from 0,5 to 5,5 be ________

A] 10 units

B] 5 units

C] 15 units

D] None of the above

] Objects are rotated around the

A] Bottom of the object

B] Base point

C] Center of the object

D] Origin

] The origin of a drawing is at

A] 0,0

B] 1,0

C] 0,1

D] 1,1

] How would you select set of objects in a drawing?

A] By a crossing window drawn from right to left

B] By a crossing window drawn left to right

C] Shift+ clicking on the objects

D] None of the above

] Fillet command can be used to obtain_________

A] Sharp corners

B] Round corners

C] Both of the above

D] None of the above

] A polar array creates new objects____

A] In a grid pattern

B] In a circular pattern

C] In a straight line

D] All of the above

] How many layers a drawing should have?

A] 1

B] 2

C] As many as depending on the complexity

D] None of the above

] Scaling objects make them______

A] Smaller

B] Bigger

C] Either smaller or bigger

D] None of the above

CNC Machining MCQ for Manufacturing Engineering

CNC Machine Tape Punch

image

248] Tape punch having 1 inch in width tape it is made by

A] Paper Mylar

B] Aluminum Mylar

C] Plastic

D] Above all

249] In point two point positioning positioning system........] Is acceptable

A] Open loop control system

B] Closed loop control system

C] Above both

D] None of them

250] In CNC machine having.......

A] Lead screw

B] Ball lead screw

C] Above both

D] None of both

CNC Program Coordinate

image

251] The aim of sub program is........

A] For find coordinates X Y Z.

B] For other small machine.

C] To avoid cutting tool nose tool nose penetration in Jobs surface of high speed.

D] While machining of job in special condition do not use time to time of program block.

252] What is mean by while while xyz co-ordinate point measure zero-measurement

A] Reference mark.

B] Work zero

C] Co-ordinate points

D] Above all

253] CNC machine specified by axis......

A] 2 axis

B] 3 axis
C] 4 axis
D] Above all
CNC Machine Axis

image

254] Xyz axis of CNC machines which point is used for measurements.
A] Work zero point
B] Machine zero point
C] Common zero point
D] Above all
255] Following which point is not useful in CNC machine.
A] various operation done on CNC machine.
B] Less amount for inspection.
C] Hard for setting measure.
D] Machine efficiency is depend upon operators skill.
256] For selection of zero offset before necessary..........
A] cutter is fixed on machine table.
B] The data entered in machine.
C] Job is fixed on machine table.
D] Speed and feed selection necessary before machine operates.
CNC Work Zero Offset Setting.

image

257] In zero offset program indicates........] Code of following

A] X y z

B] X0 y0 z00

C] X10 Y20 Z30

D] G71

258] Work zero is

A] Datum of machine zero on job position.

B] Indicate by X0Y0Z0.

C] Selection of point on job according to program.

D] The end of machining point

259] M command is used for starting operation and complete revolution cycle M03 means.

A] Stop the program.

B] Program completed and reset.

C] Complete the program.

D] Spindle clockwise motion.

CNC Machine Power Pack

image

260] CNC machine is not manually operated it is control by...........

A] Program

B] operation

C] Cam

D] Plug board system

261] In CNC machine M13 means

A] coolant stop

B] coolant on

C] spindle stop

D] coolant on & spindle on

262] The function of power pack in CNC machine.

A] For balancing of lubricants heat.

B] For increasing heat of lubricants.

C] For destroy heat of lubricant.

D] Above all.

CNC Machine Bed.

image

263] The section of CNC machine bed is.....

A] Flat

B] Half round

C] Rectangular

D] Triangular

264] Following which statement is disadvantage of CNC machine.

A] Less inspection charge.

B] Less tooling charge.

C] Increase production rate.

D] High establishment charge.

265] The point to point system is more effective for......

A] Turning

B] Profile milling

C] Grinding

D] Drilling

Tool Setting on NC Machine.

image

266] Tool setting on NC machine on......] unit.

A] Presetting device.

B] Order special device without machine.

C] On n c machine other empty time.

D] When other operation working on machine.

267] For measuring system having built-in coordinates in this system..........] is called zero position.

A] Reference point.

B] Machine zero point.

C] Work zero point

D] Program zero point.

268] Job turning on CNC machine 50 mm dia turn with programs said the trial run 50.1 mm at production time following which Idea used for correct dia making

A] by increase offset of tool 0.1 mm.

B] by increase offset of tool 0.05 mm

C] by decrease offset of tool 0.05 mm

D] by decrease offset of tool 0.1 mm

CNC Copying Lathe Machine.

image

269] For measure zero offset dim dimensions on CNC machine.........mode is set

A] MDI

B] Jog

C] Automatic

D] preset

270] Coping unit of copying lathe is work on

A] Mechanical power system

B] Hand power system

C] Hydraulic power system

D] None of them

271] Following which advantage of Pneumatic power system

A] For increase production rate.

B] Less cash for layout

C] Good climate for work

D] Above all

Principle of CNC Machine Templates.

image

272] For face copying........] Type template is used

A] Rounded

B] Plate type

C] Flat

D] Triangular

273]............] Is Main principle of CNC MACHINE?

A] Indicate all states in numbers

B] More time required for mechanical control on machine.

C] Cutting speed is more than manual control.

D] Production sequence in workshop is stored by block number in machine.

274] For copy of one shaft.......] Type template is used.

A] Rounded

B] Triangular

C] Flats

D] Square

CNC Program Tool Path.

image

275] The symptoms of continuous path is

A] Called counting system.

B] Tool and work piece on co-ordinate Axis for inter related motion.

C] By the setting of cutter feed and speed

D] Above all

276] Misc command M30 means........

A] End of program and reset

B] Program stop

C] Clockwise motion of spindle

D] Complete the programs

277] Following which affect on milling surface while by milling with unsetting spindle vertical milling machine with- longitudinal feed.

A] Convex surface

B] Concave surface

C] Radius cross line

D] Rough surface

CNC Milling Operation]

image

278] While milling by vertical milling machine with 12 mm dia end mill cutter through slot provide on mild steel plate the cutter is sleep and broken for this fault how it is avoid.

A] High speed spindle

B] Low cutting speed

C] Increase of cut depth

D] Less the depth and feed of cutter

279] Having 5 mm pitch of screw and dividing ratio of 40 : 1 what is lead of milling machine

A] 0.25 mm

B] 5 mm

C] 8 mm

D] 200 mm

280] If not use of backlash Eliminator slap cutter used for down milling operation which safety to be observed?

A] Less lead and depth

B] High lead

C] high lead and less depth

D] High lead and high speed

CNC Machine Zero & Feed Rate.

cnc machine zero.PNG

281] Zero offset is the distance between.....] And.........

A] G41 & g42

B] Machine zero & work zero

C] Reference point and tapping mode

D] None of them

282] The feed rate is programmed as mm per minute with G ....] And mm per- Revolution with G.

A] G41 & g42

B] G 43 and G 40

C] G 94 and g95

D] None of them

283] For collection all instructions from.......] In CNC control unit

A] Memory

B] Tape reader

C] Control panel

D] Operator

CNC Drilling Machine.

cnc drilling machine.jpg

284] For control forward and backward of- CNC drilling machine y axis.........

A] Spindle

B] Table

C] Clockwise

D] Column

285] M 01 command means.....

A] For stopping programs

B] End of program and reset

C] Stopping programs condition

D] Clockwise rotation of machine spindle

286] CNC machine is founded by American scientist john person in.......] Year

A] 1950

B] 1952

C] 1955

D] 1957

CNC Control, Input & Memory Unit.

cnc control.jpg

287] Name of unit used to command the CNC machine.

A] Control unit

B] Memory unit

C] Input unit

D] Output unit

288] Name of unit used to processing the data in CNC machine.

A] Memory unit

B] Control unit

C] Input unit

D] Output unit

289] Name of unit used to storing the data in CNC machine.

A] Input unit

B] Control unit

C] Memory unit

D] Output unit

Servo Motor in CNC Machine.

servo motor.jpg

290] Name of unit used to calculation of data in CNC machine.

A] Output unit

B] Arithmetic unit

C] Memory unit

D] Input unit

291] Name of unit used to display result of processing data in CNC machine

A] Arithmetic unit

B] Output unit

C] Memory unit

D] Input unit

292] Servo Motor in CNC machine is used to.............

A] Changing tool on machine spindle

B] Driving machine spindle

C] Fixing job on machine spindle

D] Proving job on spindle

Types of CNC Machine.

types of cnc.jpg

293] One of the below part of CNC machine used to changing tools on spindle.

A] Servo Motor

B] Control panel

C] Automatic tool changer A T C

D] High speed spindle

294] One of the below CNC machine in CNC milling category is.......

A] Chucking centre

B] CNC late

C] Vertical machining centre

D] Surface grinding machine

295] One of the below CNC machine in turning centre or CNC lathe category is.......

A] Vertical machining centre

B] Horizontal machining centre

C] Vertical turning centre

D] Profile grinding machine

Miscellaneous Functions for CNC Machine.

miscellaneous function.jpg

296] One of the below CNC machine in grinding Centre category is.....
A] Universal milling centre
B] Cylindrical grinding machine
C] CNC late
D] Vertical machining centre

Grinding wheels 1 grinding wheel

Grinding

297] In CNC Machine programming word M indicates
A] Feed rate
B] Spindle speed
C] Miscellaneous function
D] Tool number

298] In CNC Machine programming preparatory function G00 is for.....
A] Linear interpolation
B] Clockwise circular interpolation
C] Counter clockwise circular interpellation
D] Hold

Preparatory Functions for CNC Machine.

preparatory function.jpg

299] In CNC Machine programming preparatory function G02 is for.....

A] Linear interpolation

B] Clockwise circular interpolation

C] Counter clockwise circular interpellation

D] Hold

300] One of the bellow preparatory function G 00 is used in CNC program for.........

A] Linear interpellation or feed motion in straight line.

B] Clockwise circular interpellation

C] Point to point Positioning or Rapid motion.

D] Counter clockwise circular interpellation

301] One of the bellow preparatory function used in CNC program for 3D interpellation

A] G 05

B] G12

C] G17

D] G18

Threading & Tapping on CNC Machine.

threading & tapping on cnc.jpg

302] One of the bellow preparatory you function used in CNC program for thread cutting constant lead

A] G33

B] G40

C] G53

D] G62

303] One of the bellow preparatory function used in CNC program for tapping operation.

A] G-40

B] G53

C] G62

D] G63

304] One of the below preparatory function used in CNC program for milling operation.

A] G62

B] G63

C] G 78, 79

D] G81

Drilling, Boring & Reaming on CNC Machine

drilling boring & reaming.jpg

305] One of the bellow preparatory function used in CNC program for drilling operation.

A] G 81

B] G 82

C] G 84

D] G 85

306] One of the bellow preparatory function used in CNC program for reaming operation.

A] G 84

B] G 85

C] G 86

D] G 90

307] Onc of the below preparatory function used in CNC program for boring operation.

A] G 86

B] G 90

C] G 91

D] G 92

CNC Program Sequence Number.

cnc program sequence.png

308] In CNC program which letter is used to indicate the sequence number of the block

A] N

B] G

C] F

D] S

309] In CNC program which letter is used to indicate position of linear axis

A] ABC

B] UVW

C] XYZ

D] IJK

310] One of the below letters used in CNC program for Feed rate

A] S

B] F

C] T

D] M

Tool Change & Spindle Speed in CNC Machine.

tool change i cnc.jpg

311] One of the below letters used in CNC program for spindle speed in

RPM

A] M

B] T

C] S

D] F

312] In CNC program which letter is used to indicate TOOL function number of tool

A] T

B] S

C] M

D] F

313] In CNC program which miscellaneous function used to program stop

A] M03

B] M00

C] M01

D] M02

CNC Machine Spindle Direction.

cnc machine spindle direction.png

314] One of the below miscellaneous function used to program optional Stop

A] M 01

B] M 02

C] M 03

D] M 04

315] In CNC program miscellaneous function M02 is used to......

A] Program stop

B] Optional program stop

C] End of program

D] Clockwise spindle on

316] In CNC program miscellaneous function M03 is used to..........

A] Counter clockwise spindle on

B] Clockwise spindle on

C] Spindle off

D] Tool change

Coolant in CNC Machine.

coolant in cnc machine.jpg

317] One of the below miscellaneous function used in CNC program for spindle stop.

A] M04

B] M05

C] M06

D] M07

318] In CNC program which miscellaneous function is used for Tools change

A] M06

B] M07

C] M09

D] M10

319] One of the below miscellaneous function used in CNC program for coolant on

A] M08

B] M09

C] M10

D] M11

Clamping the Job on CNC Machine.

clamping the job on
cnc.jpg

320] One of the below miscellaneous function in CNC program used for coolant off

A] M11

B] M10

<u>C] M9</u>

D] M15

321] In CNC program which miscellaneous function used for clamping the job on machine table.

A] M09

<u>B] M10</u>

C] M11

D] M15

322] One of the below miscellaneous function in CNC program used for unclamp the job

<u>A] M11</u>

B] M15

C] M30

D] M60

<u>Work piece change in CNC Machine.</u>

workpice change in cnc.jpg

323] In CNC program which miscellaneous function used for change of workpiece

A] M30

<u>B] M60</u>

C] M68

D] M78

324] The machine is.........for zero off-setting on CNC Machine.

A] In MDI Mode

B] In JOG Mode

C] In Automatic Mode

D] In Present Mode

325] The feed rate on NC Machine is indicate by ......code.

A] X

B] Y

C] F

D] Z

CNC Machine Axis Position]

cnc machine axis position.jpg

326] The position of axis is indicate by.......code.

A] X,Y,Z

B] P,Q,R

C] A,B,C

D] M,N,O

327] CNC Drilling Machine is on.......Axis Programmed.

A] Two Axis

B] Three Axis

C] Four Axis

D] Six Axis

328] From.......unit collect instruction in control unit of CNC

A] Machine Tool

B] Instruction

C] Magnetic Box

D] Memory

Working Graph of CNC Machine]

working graph of cnc machine.jpg

329] For preparing tape of NC Machine----------code is used.

A] EIA Code

B] ISO Code

C] ASC Code

D] None of them.

330] CNC Machine gives more accurate production than convention machine, But it is more expensive because.

A] It has AC cabin

B] It has dust proof cabin

C] It has strong foundation

D] It has more space

331] CNC Machine is working on graphical base the point on digital line, indicated digital points call..........

A] Graph

B] Input Media

C] Co-Ordinate

D] Original Point

Axis Rotary Motion in CNC Machine]

axis rotary motion in CNC.png

332] On CNC Machine for longitudinal feed has.......axes, cross feed......axis and for vertical feed........axis name given.

A] A,B,C

B] X,Y,Z

C] P,Q,R

D] M,N,O

333] For rotary motion CNC machine axis has.......name given.

A] A,B,C

B] X,Y,Z

C] P,Q,R

D] M,N,O

334] CNC Machine means.......

A] Natural Control Machine

B] Pneumatic control Machine

C] Numerical Control Machine

D] No Command Machine

Basic Computer Skills MCQ for Manufacturing Engineering

1] WWW stands for ?

A] World Whole Web

B] Wide World Web

C] Web World Wide

D] World Wide Web

2] Which of the following are components of Central Processing Unit (CPU) ?

A] Arithmetic logic unit, Mouse

B] Arithmetic logic unit, Control unit

C] Arithmetic logic unit, Integrated Circuits

D] Control Unit, Monitor

3] Which among following first generation of computers had ?

A] Vaccum Tubes and Magnetic Drum

B] Integrated Circuits

C] Magnetic Tape and Transistors

D] All of above

4] Where is RAM located ?

A] Expansion Board

B] External Drive

C] Mother Board

D] All of above

5] If a computer has more than one processor then it is known as ?

A] Uniprocess

B] Multiprocessor

C] Multithreaded

D] Multiprogramming

6] If a computer provides database services to other, then it will be known as ?

A] Web server

B] Application server

C] Database server

D] FTP server

7] Full form of URL is ?

A] Uniform Resource Locator

B] Uniform Resource Link

C] Uniform Registered Link

D] Unified Resource Link

8] In which of the following form, data is stored in computer ?

A] Decimal

B] Binary

C] HexaDecimal

D] Octal

9] Technology used to provide internet by transmitting data over wires of telephone network is ?

A] Transmitter

B] Diodes

C] HHL

D] DSL

10] Which level language is Assembly Language ?
A] high-level programming language
B] medium-level programming language
C] low-level programming language
D] machine language
11] Documents, Movies, Images and Photographs etc are stored at a ?
A] Application Sever
B] Web Sever
C] Print Server
D] File Server
12] Which of following is used in RAM ?
A] Conductor
B] Semi Conductor
C] Vaccum Tubes
D] Transistor
13] What is full form of GUI in terms of computers ?
A] Graphical user Instrument
B] Graphical unified Interface
C] Graphical unified Instrument
D] Graphical user Interface
14] What is full form of ALU ?
A] Arithmetic logic unit
B] Allowed logic unit
C] Ascii logic unit
D] Arithmetic least unit
15] Who was the Founder of Bluetooth ?
A] Ericson
B] Martin Cooper
C] Steve Jobs
D] Apple
16] Who was the father of Internet ?
A] Chares Babbage
B] Vint Cerf
C] Denis Riche
D] Martin Cooper
17] Verification is process of ?
A] Access
B] Login

C] Logout

D] Authentication

18] What is LINUX ?

A] Malware

B] Operating System

C] Application Program

D] Firmware

19] What is the name of first super computer of India ?

A] Saga 220

B] PARAM 8000

C] ENIAC

D] PARAM 6000

20] Which is most common language used in web designing ?

A] C

B] C++

C] PHP

D] HTML

21] Who is also known as Father of Computer ?

A] Vint Cerf

B] Tim Berner Lee

C] Charles Babbage

D] Steve Jobs

Machine Kinematics for Manufacturing Engineering

1. The unit of linear acceleration is

a) kg-m

b) m/s

c) m/s2

d) rad/s2

2. The angular velocity (in rad/s) of a body rotating at N r.p.m. is

a) π N/60

b) 2 π N/60

c) π N/120

d) π N/180

3. The linear velocity of a body rotating at ω rad/s along a circular path of radius r is given by

a) ω.r

b) ω/r

c) ωs2.r
d) ωs2/r

4. When a particle moves along a straight path, then the particle has
a) tangential acceleration only
b) centripetal acceleration only
c) both tangential and centripetal acceleration
d) none of the mentioned

5. When a particle moves with a uniform velocity along a circular path, then the particle has
a) tangential acceleration only
b) centripetal acceleration only
c) both tangential and centripetal acceleration
d) none of the mentioned

6. When the motion of a body is confined to only one plane, the motion is said to be
a) plane motion
b) rectilinear motion
c) curvilinear Motion
d) none of the mentioned

7. ________________ is the simplest type of motion and is along a straight line path.
a) plane motion
b) rectilinear motion
c) curvilinear Motion
d) none of the mentioned

8. __________________ is the motion along a curved path.
a) plane motion
b) rectilinear motion
c) curvilinear Motion
d) none of the mentioned

9. Displacement of a body is a ____________ quantity.
a) scalar
b) vector
c) scalar and vector
d) none of the mentioned

10. A train covers 60 miles between 2 p.m. and 4 p.m. How fast was it going at 3 p.m.?
a) 60 mph

b) 30 mph

c) 40 mph

d) 50 mph

11. The force which acts along the radius of a circle and directed ______________ the centre of the circle is known as centripetal force.

a) away from

b) towards

c) at the

d) none of the mentioned

12. The unit of mass moment of inertia in S.I. units is

a) m4

b) kgf-m-s2

c) kg-m2

d) N-m

13. Joule is a unit of

a) force

b) work

c) power

d) none of the mentioned

14. The energy possessed by a body, for doing work by virtue of its position, is called

a) potential energy

b) kinetic energy

c) electrical energy

d) chemical energy

15. When a body of mass moment of inertia I (about a given axis) is rotated about that axis with an angular velocity, then the kinetic energy of rotation is

a) 0.5 I.ω

b) I.ω

c) 0.5 I.ω2

d) I.ω2

16. The wheels of a moving car possess

a) potential energy only

b) kinetic energy of translation only

c) kinetic energy of rotation only

d) kinetic energy of translation and rotation both.

17. The bodies which rebound after impact are called

a) inelastic bodies

b) elastic bodies

c) solid bodies

d) none of the mentioned

18. The coefficient of restitution for inelastic bodies is

a) zero

b) between zero and one

c) one

d) more than one

19. Which of the following statement is correct ?

a) The kinetic energy of a body during impact remains constant.

b) The kinetic energy of a body before impact is equal to the kinetic energy of a body after impact.

c) The kinetic energy of a body before impact is less than the kinetic energy of a body after impact.

d) The kinetic energy of a body before impact is more than the kinetic energy of a body after impact.

20. A body of mass m moving with a constant velocity v strikes another body of same mass m moving with same velocity but in opposite direction. The common velocity of both the bodies after collision is

a) v

b) 2 v

c) 4 v

d) 8 v

Machine Dynamics for Manufacturing Engineering

1. A disc is spinning with an angular velocity ? rad/s about the axis of spin. The couple applied to the disc causing precession will be

a) 1/2Iω2

b) Iω2

c) 1/2 Iω ωp

d) Iω ωp

2. A disc spinning on its axis at 20 rad/s will undergo precession when a torque 100 N-m is applied about an axis normal to it at an angular speed, if mass moment of inertia of the disc is the 1 kg-m2

a) 2 rad/s

b) 5 rad/s

c) 10 rad/s

d) 20 rad/s

3. The engine of an aeroplane rotates in clockwise direction when seen from the tail end and the aeroplane takes a turn to the left. The effect of the gyroscopic couple on the aeroplane will be

a) to raise the nose and dip the tail
b) to dip the nose and raise the tail
c) to raise the nose and tail
d) to dip the nose and tail

4. The air screw of an aeroplane is rotating clockwise when looking from the front. If it makes a left turn, the gyroscopic effect will

a) tend to depress the nose and raise the tail
b) tend to raise the nose and depress the tail
c) tilt the aeroplane
d) none of the mentioned

5. The rotor of a ship rotates in clockwise direction when viewed from the stern and the ship takes a left turn. The effect of the gyroscopic couple acting on it will be

a) to raise the bow and stern
b) to lower the bow and stern
c) to raise the bow and lower the stern
d) to lower the bow and raise the stern

6. When the pitching of a ship is upward, the effect of gyroscopic couple acting on it will be

a) to move the ship towards port side
b) to move the ship towards star-board
c) to raise the bow and lower the stern
d) to raise the stern and lower the bow

7. In an automobile, if the vehicle makes a left turn, the gyroscopic torque

a) increases the forces on the outer wheels
b) decreases the forces on the outer wheels
c) does not affect the forces on the outer wheels
d) none of the mentioned

8. A motor car moving at a certain speed takes a left turn in a curved path. If the engine rotates in the same direction as that of wheels, then due to the centrifugal forces

a) the reaction on the inner wheels increases and on the outer wheels decreases

b) the reaction on the outer wheels increases and on the inner wheels decreases

c) the reaction on the front wheels increases and on the rear wheels decreases

d) the reaction on the rear wheels increases and on the front wheels decreases

9. A uniform disc of diameter 300 mm and of mass 5 kg is mounted on one end of an arm of length 600 mm. The other end of the arm is free to rotate in a universal bearing. If the disc rotates about the arm with a speed of 300 r.p.m. clockwise, looking from the front, with what speed will it precess about the vertical axis?

a) 14.7 rad/s

b) 15.7 rad/s

c) 16.7 rad/s

d) 17.7 rad/s

10. An aeroplane makes a complete half circle of 50 metres radius, towards left, when flying at 200 km per hr. The rotary engine and the propeller of the plane has a mass of 400 kg and a radius of gyration of 0.3 m. The engine rotates at 2400 r.p.m. clockwise when viewed from the rear. Find the gyroscopic couple on the aircraft.

a) 10.046 kN-m

b) 11.046 kN-m

c) 12.046 kN-m

d) 13.046 kN-m

11. The turbine rotor of a ship has a mass of 8 tonnes and a radius of gyration 0.6 m. It rotates at 1800 r.p.m. clockwise, when looking from the stern. Determine the gyroscopic couple, if the ship travels at 100 km/hr and steer to the left in a curve of 75 m radius.

a) 100.866 kN-m

b) 200.866 kN-m

c) 300.866 kN-m

d) 400.866 kN-m

12. The heavy turbine rotor of a sea vessel rotates at 1500 r.p.m. clockwise looking from the stern, its mass being 750 kg. The vessel pitches with an angular velocity of 1 rad/s. Determine the gyroscopic couple transmitted to the hull when bow is rising, if the radius of gyration for the rotor is 250 mm.

a) 4.364 kN-m

b) 5.364 kN-m
c) 6.364 kN-m
d) 7.364 kN-m

13. The turbine rotor of a ship has a mass of 3500 kg. It has a radius of gyration of 0.45 m and a speed of 3000 r.p.m. clockwise when looking from stern. Determine the gyroscopic couple upon the ship when the ship is steering to the left on a curve of 100 m radius at a speed of 36 km/h.

a) 11.27 kN-m
b) 22.27 kN-m
c) 33.27 kN-m
d) 44.27 kN-m

14. The turbine rotor of a ship has a mass of 3500 kg. It has a radius of gyration of 0.45 m and a speed of 3000 r.p.m. clockwise when looking from stern. Determine the gyroscopic couple upon the ship when the ship is pitching in a simple harmonic motion, the bow falling with its maximum velocity. The period of pitching is 40 seconds and the total angular displacement between the two extreme positions of pitching is 12 degrees.

a) 3.675 kN-m
b) 4.675 kN-m
c) 5.675 kN-m
d) 6.675 kN-m

15. The mass of the turbine rotor of a ship is 20 tonnes and has a radius of gyration of 0.60 m. Its speed is 2000 r.p.m. The ship pitches 6° above and 6° below the horizontal position. A complete oscillation takes 30 seconds and the motion is simple harmonic. Determine Maximum gyroscopic couple.

a) 11.185 kN-m
b) 22.185 kN-m
c) 33.185 kN-m
d) 44.185 kN-m

16. The mass of the turbine rotor of a ship is 20 tonnes and has a radius of gyration of 0.60 m. Its speed is 2000 r.p.m. The ship pitches 6° above and 6° below the horizontal position. A complete oscillation takes 30 seconds and the motion is simple harmonic. Determine Maximum angular acceleration of the ship during pitching.

a) 0.0016 rad/s2
b) 0.0026 rad/s2
c) 0.0036 rad/s2

d) 0.0046 rad/s2

17. A ship propelled by a turbine rotor which has a mass of 5 tonnes and a speed of 2100 r.p.m. The rotor has a radius of gyration of 0.5 m and rotates in a clockwise direction when viewed from the stern. Find the gyroscopic effect when the ship sails at a speed of 30 km/h and steers to the left in a curve having 60 m radius.

a) 38.5 kN-m
b) 48.5 kN-m
c) 58.5 kN-m
d) 68.5 kN-m

18. A ship propelled by a turbine rotor which has a mass of 5 tonnes and a speed of 2100 r.p.m. The rotor has a radius of gyration of 0.5 m and rotates in a clockwise direction when viewed from the stern. Find the gyroscopic effect when the ship pitches 6 degree above and 6 degree below the horizontal position. The bow is descending with its maximum velocity. The motion due to pitching is simple harmonic and the periodic time is 20 seconds.

a) 6075 N-m
b) 7075 N-m
c) 8075 N-m
d) 9075 N-m

Thermodynamics for Manufacturing Engineering

1. A piston/cylinder with a cross-sectional area of 0.01 m^2 is resting on the stops. With an outside pressure of 100 kPa, what should be the water pressure to lift the piston?

a) 178kPa
b) 188kPa
c) 198kPa
d) 208kPa

3. A large exhaust fan in a lab room keeps the pressure inside at 10 cm water relative vacuum to the hallway? What is the net force acting on the door measuring 1.9 m by 1.1 m?

a) 2020 N
b) 2030 N
c) 2040 N
d) 2050 N

4. A 5 m long vertical tube having cross sectional area 200 cm^2 is placed in a water. It is filled with 15°C water, with the bottom closed and the top

open to 100 kPa atmosphere. How much water is present in tube?

a) 99.9 kg
b) 109.9 kg
c) 89.9 kg
d) 79.9 kg

5. A 5 m long vertical tube having cross sectional area 200 cm2 is placed in a water. It is filled with 15°C water, with the bottom closed and the top open to 100 kPa atmosphere. What is the pressure at the bottom of tube ?

a) 119 kPa
b) 129 kPa
c) 139 kPa
d) 149 kPa

6. Find the pressure of water at 200°C and having specific volume of 1.5 m3/kg.

a) 0.9578 m3/kg
b) 0.8578 m3/kg
c) 0.7578 m3/kg
d) 0.6578 m3/kg

7. Find the pressure of water at 200°C and having specific volume of 1.5 m^3/kg.

a) 141.6 kPa
b) 111.6 kPa
c) 121.6 kPa
d) 161.6 kPa

8. A 5m^3 container is filled with 840 kg of granite (density is 2400 kg/m^3) and the rest of the volume is air (density is 1.15 kg/m^3). Find the mass of air present in the container.

a) 9.3475 kg
b) 8.3475 kg
c) 6.3475 kg
d) 5.3475 kg

9. A 100 m tall building receives superheated steam at 200 kPa at ground and leaves saturated vapour from the top at 125 kPa by losing 110 kJ/kg of heat. What should be the minimum inlet temperature at the ground of the building so that no steam will condense inside the pipe at steady state?

a) 363.54°C
b) 263.54°C
c) 163.54°C

d) none of the mentioned

10. The pressure gauge on an air tank shows 60 kPa when the diver is 8 m down in the ocean. At what depth will the gauge pressure be zero?

a) 34.118 m

b) 24.118 m

c) 14.118 m

d) none of the mentioned

11. A piston-cylinder device initially contains air at 150 kPa and 27°C. At this state, the volume is 400 litre. The mass of the piston is such that a 350 kPa pressure is required to move it. The air is now heated until its volume has doubled. Determine the final temperature.

a) 1400 K

b) 400 K

c) 500 K

d) 1500 K

12. A piston-cylinder device initially contains air at 150 kPa and 27°C. At this state, the volume is 400 litre. The mass of the piston is such that a 350 kPa pressure is required to move it. The air is now heated until its volume has doubled. Determine work done by the air.

a) 120 kJ

b) 130 kJ

c) 100 kJ

d) 140 kJ

13. Find the change in u for carbon dioxide between 600 K and 1200 K for a constant Cv0 value.

a) 291.8 kJ/kg

b) 391.8 kJ/kg

c) 491.8 kJ/kg

d) 591.8 kJ/kg

14. Calculate the change in enthalpy of carbon dioxide from 30 to 1500°C at 100 kPa at constant specific heat.

a) 2237.7 kJ/kg

b) 1637.7 kJ/kg

c) 1237.7 kJ/kg

d) 2337.7 kJ/kg

15. A sealed rigid vessel has volume of 1 m3 and contains 2 kg of water at 100°C. The vessel is now heated. If a safety pressure valve is installed, at what pressure should the valve be set to have a maximum temperature of

200°C ?

a) <u>431.3 kPa</u>

b) 531.3 kPa

c) 631.3 kPa

d) 731.3 kPa

16. A system undergoing change in state from A to B along path 'X' receives 100 J heat and does 40 J work. It returns to state A from B along path 'Y' with work input of 30 J. Calculate the heat transfer involved along the path 'Y'.

a) – 60 J

b) 60 J

c) <u>– 90 J</u>

d) 90 J

17. Which of the following were used as fixed points before 1954?

a) The ice point

b) The steam point

c) <u>All of the mentioned</u>

d) None of the mentioned

18. What is the standard fixed point of thermometry?

a) The ice point

b) The steam point

c) <u>The triple point of water</u>

d) None of the mentioned

19. All gases and vapours approach ideal gas behaviour at?

a) High pressure and high density

b) <u>Low pressure and low density</u>

c) High pressure and low density

d) Low pressure and high density

20. The value of ratio of the steam point temperature to the ice point temperature is?

a) 1.466

b) 1.266

c) 1.166

d) <u>1.366</u>

21. Celsius temperature of the triple point of water is (in degree Celsius)?

a) -0.00

b) 0.00

c) 0.01

d) None of the mentioned

22. Which of the following is chosen as the standard thermometric substance?

a) Gas

b) Liquid

c) Solid

d) All of the mentioned

23. A real gas behaves as an ideal gas when?

a) Temperature approaches zero

b) Pressure approaches zero

c) Both temperature and pressure approaches zero

d) None of the mentioned

24. The temperature interval from the oxygen point to the gold point is divided into how many parts?

a) 2

b) 3

c) 4

d) 1

Fluid Mechanics MCQ for Manufacturing Engineering

1. Which one is in a state of failure?

a) Solid

b) Liquid

c) Gas

d) Fluid

2. A small shear force is applied on an element and then removed. If the element regains it's original position, what kind of an element can it be?

a) Solid

b) Liquid

c) Fluid

d) Gaseous

3. In which type of matter, one won't find a free surface?

a) Solid

b) Liquid

c) Gas

d) Fluid

4. If a person studies about a fluid which is at rest, what will you call his domain of study?

a) Fluid Mechanics
b) Fluid Statics
c) Fluid Kinematics
d) Fluid Dynamics
5. The value of the compressibility of an ideal fluid is
a) zero
b) unity
c) infinity
d) more than that of a real fluid
6. The value of the Bulk Modulus of an ideal fluid is
a) zero
b) unity
c) infinity
d) less than that of a real fluid
7. The value of the viscosity of an ideal fluid is
a) zero
b) unity
c) infinity
d) more than that of a real fluid
8. The value of the surface tension of an ideal fluid is
a) zero
b) unity
c) infinity
d) more than that of a real fluid

9. Which of the following statement is true about vapor pressure of a liquid?

a) Vapor pressure is closely related to molecular activity and temperature of the liquid

b) Vapor pressure is closely related to molecular activity but independent of the temperature of the liquid

c) Vapor pressure is not affected by molecular activity and temperature of the liquid

d) Vapor pressure is not affected by molecular activity and is independent of the temperature of the liquid

10. Which of the following equation correctly depicts the relation between the vapor pressure of a liquid and it's temperature?

a) Vapor pressure increases linearly with the increase in temperature of the liquid

b) Vapor pressure increases slightly with the increase in temperature of the liquid at low temperatures and the rate of increase goes high at higher temperatures

c) Vapor pressure increases rapidly with the increase in temperature of the liquid at low temperatures and the rate of increase goes low at higher temperatures

d) Vapor pressure remains unchanged with the increase in temperature of the liquid

11. Which of the following is the condition for the boiling of a liquid?

a) Absolute pressure of a liquid must be greater than or equal to it's vapor pressure

b) Absolute pressure of a liquid must be less than or equal to it's vapor pressure

c) Absolute pressure of a liquid must be equal to it's vapor pressure

d) Absolute pressure of a liquid must be greater than it's vapor pressure

12. Which of the following machines have the possibility of cavitation?

a) Reaction turbines and centrifugal pumps

b) Reaction turbines and reciprocating pumps

c) Impulse turbines and centrifugal pumps

d) Impulse turbines and reciprocating pumps

13. The three liquids 1, 2, and 3 with vapor pressures V1, V2 and V3 respectively, are kept under same pressure. If V1 > V2 > V3, which liquid will start boiling early?

a) liquid 1

b) liquid 2

c) liquid 3

d) they will start boiling at the same time

14. Equal amount of a particular liquid is poured into three similar containers, namely 1, 2 and 3, at a temperature of T1, T2 and T3 respectively. If T1 < T2 < T3, the liquid in which container will have the highest vapor pressure?

a) container 1

b) container 2

c) container 3

d) the vapor pressure of the liquid will remain the same irrespective of it's temperature

15. The absolute pressure of a water is 0.5kN above it's vapor pressure. If it flows with a velocity of 1m/s, what will be the value of Cavitation

Number describing the flow induced boiling?

a) 0.25

b) 0.5

c) 1

d) 2

16. Which of the following is correct regarding the formation and collapse of vapor bubbles in a liquid?

a) Vapor bubbles are formed when the fluid pressure goes above the vapor pressure and collapses when the fluid pressure goes above the bubble pressure

b) Vapor bubbles are formed when the fluid pressure goes above the vapor pressure and collapses when the fluid pressure goes below the bubble pressure

c) Vapor bubbles are formed when the fluid pressure drops below the vapor pressure and collapses when the fluid pressure goes below the bubble pressure

d) Vapor bubbles are formed when the fluid pressure drops below the vapor pressure and collapses when the fluid pressure goes above the bubble pressure

www.ingramcontent.com/pod-product-compliance
Ingram Content Group UK Ltd.
Pitfield, Milton Keynes, MK11 3LW, UK
UKHW021911190726
13853UKWH00002B/621